C000166136

The Random Book of...

MICHAEL

Dan Tester

The Random Book of...

MICHAEL

Well, I didn't know that!

All statistics, facts and figures are correct as of March 31st 2009.

© Dan Tester
Dan Tester has asserted his rights in accordance with the
Copyright, Designs and Patents Act 1988 to be identified
as the author of this work.

Published By:

Stripe Publishing Ltd
First Floor, 3 St. Georges Place, Brighton, BN1 4GA

Email: info@stripepublishing.co.uk
Web: www.stripepublishing.co.uk

First published 2009

A catalogue record for this book is available from the British Library.

10-digit ISBN: 1-907158-00-6
13-digit ISBN: 978-1-907158-00-1

Printed and bound by Gutenberg Press Ltd., Malta.

Editor: Dan Tester
Illustrations: Jonathan Pugh (www.pughcartoons.co.uk)
Typesetting: Andrew Searle
Cover: Andy Heath

To everyone called Michael, and KC

Dan Tester – March 2009

INTRODUCTION

Michael is an immensely popular name, especially in the United States of America where there are over 3,000,000 of them!

Not as rife in the United Kingdom, Michael has still featured heavily on the baby name lists of prospective parents for hundreds of years.

To me, the name has always had an aura of authority and respectability. A headmaster at my primary school was called Michael and one of my earliest heroes was Michael Robinson after he scored the goal that fired my beloved Brighton & Hove Albion to Wembley for the first time in 1983.

This was just a few years after being dazzled by Michael Jackson, musically.

It's a name whose popularity may be waning as Jacks, Zacks, Ollies and Joshs rampage through the playground but Micks, Mickeys and Michaels have done more than enough to cement their places in history.

I salute you all!

Dan Tester – March 2009

WHERE DOES MICHAEL COME FROM?

Michael or Micha'el comes from Hebrew: לאכים / לָאְכִים (mee-KHA-el), meaning 'Who is like God?'

The name first appears in the Bible – Numbers 13 verse 13 – where Sethur the son of Michael is one of twelve spies sent into the Land of Canaan.

The Archangel Michael, referred to later in the Bible – Daniel 12 verse 1 – is considered a saint by the Roman Catholic Church.

In English it is sometimes shortened to Mike or, especially in Ireland, Mick or Micky.

Female forms of Michael include Michelle and Michaela, although there are women with the name Michael, such as Michael Learned…

Michael Learned is a four-time Emmy-winning and Golden Globe-nominated American actress who is best known for her role as Olivia Walton (the mother) in *The Waltons*.

She was billed as 'Miss Michael Learned' as she was relatively unknown at the time. The producers did not want to confuse viewers about her gender.

Surnames that derive from Michael include MacMichael, McMichael, Micallef, Michaelson, Mitchell, Dimichele and Carmichael.

Michael first appeared in the Top Ten of first names in England
and Wales in the 1930s and was a regular feature until the 1990s...

	Michael	Most popular
1930s	7th	John
1940s	3rd	John
1950s	4th	David
1960s	6th	David
1970s	9th	Paul
1980s	5th	Christopher

Michael across the globe:

Arabic:	ميخائيل / ميكائيل
Armenia:	Միքայել (Mikayel)
Bulgaria:	Михаил (Mihail)
Catalan:	Miquel
Croatia:	Mihael or Mihovil
Czech Republic:	Michal
Denmark:	Mikkel
Estonia:	Mihkel
France:	Michel
Gaelic:	Micheal
Georgia:	მიხეილ (Mikheil)
Greece:	Μιχαήλ (Mikhaēl)
Holland:	Michiel
Hebrew:	מיכאל (Mikha'el)
Hungary:	Mihály
Ireland:	Mícheál
Italy:	Michele
Macedonia:	Михаил (Mihail)

Poland:	Micha
Portugal:	Miguel
Romania:	Mihai
Russia:	Михаил (Mikha'il)
Serbia:	Михајло (Mihajlo)
Slovakia:	Michal
Spain:	Miguel
Sweden:	Mikael
Turkey:	Mikail
Ukraine:	Михайло (Mykháylo)
Wales:	Mihangel

"One day sir, you may tax it."
Michael Faraday*'s reply to William Gladstone, then British Minister of Finance, when asked of the practical value of electricity.*

INTERNATIONAL ONE-CAP WONDER MICHAELS

England
Michael Whitham 05/03/1892 Ireland 0-2 England
Michael Phelan 15/11/1989 England 0-0 Italy
Michael Ball 28/02/2001 England 3-0 Spain
Michael Ricketts 13/02/2002 Holland 1-1 England

Scotland
Michael Dunbar 20/03/1886 N. Ire. 2-7 Scotland
Michael Gilhooley 04/02/1922 Wales 2-1 Scotland
Michael Cullen 02/05/1956 Scotland 1-1 Austria

REAL MICHAELS

Billy Idol's real name is **William Michael Albert Broad**. He was expelled from the St. Mary's cub scouts in Goring-by-Sea, West Sussex, for kissing a young girl behind a hotdog stand.

He became part of a Sex Pistols fan club called the Bromley Contingent in the mid-seventies and on forming the band Chelsea changed his name to Bill Idol after remembering a comment a teacher had written on a report card; 'William is idle'.

Christian Michael Leonard Hawkins is the real name of the American actor Christian Slater who starred in *Robin Hood Prince of Thieves, Mobsters* and *True Romance*.

Pint-sized actor **Danny Michael DeVito Junior** was born in 1944 and became a household name playing acerbic and moral-less Louie De Palma, boss of the Sunshine Cab Company in the hit U.S. sitcom *Taxi*.

He has three children with Rhea Perlman, famous for her Carla Tortelli character in the American comedy *Cheers*, and once claimed to have had sex in every possible place in the Lincoln Bedroom at the White House.

Michael Peter Balzary was born in Melbourne, Australia in 1962. 'Flea' formed the Red Hot Chili

Peppers with Los Angeles high school friends Anthony Kiedis and Jack Irons in the early eighties and scored huge critical successes with Blood Sugar Sex Magik (1995) Californication (1999), By the Way (2002) and Stadium Arcadium (2006). His second daughter, Sunny Bebop, was born in 2005.

Georgios Kyriacos Panayiotou formed Wham! with best friend Andrew Ridgeley in 1981 and took the pop world by storm with a string of number ones including Wake Me Up Before You Go Go, Careless Whisper and Everything She Wants. **George Michael** received £1.5 million for performing a one hour concert in Moscow for the 300 guests of Russian billionaire Vladimir Potanin on New Year's Eve 2006. The previous performance by the half Greek-Cypriot singer was a free gig for nurses in North London.

John Wayne was born Marion Robert Morrison in Winterset, Iowa in 1907. His parents decided to change his name to **Marion Michael Morrison** after they chose to name their next son Robert.

Wayne was married three times, all of them Hispanic women. A relatively large number of the cast and crew of Wayne's 1956 film *The Conqueror* – shot in south-western Utah, generally downwind from where the U.S. Government had tested nuclear weapons in south-eastern Nevada – developed various forms of cancer.

Sir Maurice Joseph Micklewhite, Jr. (b. 1933) originally decided on the stage name of **Michael Scott**. In a telephone box in Leicester Square, **Michael Caine** called his agent who explained that the name was already in use. The young actor scanned around for inspiration and saw a sign for the 1954 film, *The Caine Mutiny*, a drama set during World War II that starred Humphrey Bogart.

The Oscar-winning actor – Best Actor in a Supporting Role for *Hannah and Her Sisters* (1986) and *The Cider House Rules* (1999) – once joked to an interviewer that had he looked the other way, he would have ended up as "Michael One Hundred and One Dalmatians".

The *Beetlejuice* and *Batman* actor **Michael Keaton** was actually christened **Michael Douglas**. As *The Streets of San Francisco* star rose to prominence, he changed his name – to adhere to Screen Actors Guild (SAG) rules – in 1979 after reading an article on actress Diane Keaton.

As at the end of 2008, Joe Yule Jr., born **Mickey Rooney** (b. 1920), had starred in more than 170 films, been married eight times and fathered nine children.

Rooney claimed that after meeting Walt Disney the cartoonist was inspired to name **Mickey Mouse** after him, although Disney himself always stated that he had changed the name from 'Mortimer Mouse' on the suggestion of his wife.

Michel Demetri Chalhoub (Arabic: عمر الشريف)
converted to Islam in 1955 in order to marry Egyptian
actress Faten Hamama and took the name Omar al-Sharif.
The actor is fluent in Arabic, English, Greek and French,
and also speaks Italian and Turkish.

The infamous Ozzy Osbourne was born **Jonathan
Michael Osborne** on December 3rd 1948 in
Birmingham, England and is the lead vocalist of the heavy
metal band Black Sabbath.

Married to *X Factor* judge and former band manager
Sharon, the singer once said: "I was taking drugs so much I
was a wreck. The final straw came when I shot all our cats.
We had about 17, and I went crazy and shot them all. My
wife found me under the piano in a white suit, a shotgun in
one hand and a knife in the other."

Paul Michael Levesque is an American professional
wrestler. His stage name Triple H is an abbreviation of his
former ring name, Hunter Hearst Helmsley.

Since wrestling for the Raw brand of World Wrestling
Entertainment (WWE), the New Hampshire-born man-
mountain has been world champion 11 times: a six-time WWE
Champion and a five-time World Heavyweight Champion.

Tom Berenger – **Thomas Michael Moore**
Mickey Rourke – Philip Andre Rourke, Jr.
Mickey Spillane – Frank Morrison Spillane

Midge Ure – James Ure. Midge is a phonetic reversal of his real name, Jim.

Trent Reznor – **Michael Trent Reznor** (Nine Inch Nails)

⏤⏤◆⏤⏤

MUSICAL MICHAELS

The Beatles' Sergeant Pepper album sleeve featured a doll wearing a 'Welcome the Rolling Stones' T-shirt photographed by **Michael Cooper**. This was reciprocated by hiding the Fab Four in the undergrowth on the Stones' cover of Satanic Majesties Request.

Stage name	**real name:**
Michael Bolton	Michael Bolotin
Clown (Slipknot)	Michael Shawn Crahan
Mickey Dolenz (The Monkees)	George Michael Braddock
Black Francis (Pixies)	Charles Michael Kittridge Thompson IV
Mick Jagger	Michael Phillip Jagger
Tony Orlando (Dawn)	Michael Anthony Orlando Cassivitis
Ozzy Osbourne	John Michael Osbourne
Michael Stipe (R.E.M.)	John Michael Stipe
Zim Zum (Life, Sex & Death, Marilyn Manson)	Timothy Michael Linton

G4 finished second in the first ever series of *The X-Factor* in 2004. The four-piece vocal group included **Michael Christie** – born April 21st 1981 – who speaks fluent Swedish. The band split in 2007.

Michael Lachowski is the bass player for Pylon. The new wave band formed when four art students met at the University of Georgia in the US. In December 1987, REM was chosen by Rolling Stone as "America's Best Rock And Roll Band," an honour that was quickly dismissed by drummer Bill Berry.

"Pylon are much more deserving of the accolade."

Michael Rabinowitz is most famous for bringing bassoon into the jazz genre. He has recorded with Red Rodney, John Hicks, Ira Sullivan, Wynton Marsalis, Dave Douglas and Joe Lovano. He is head of the band Bassoon in the Wild.

Michael Jackson – born in Gary, Indiana, USA August 29th 1958, died June 25th, 2009, Los Angeles – debuted at the age of five as a member of the Jackson 5 and went on to become a pop megastar as a solo artist dominating the charts from the late 1970s to the mid-1990s.

The album Thriller, released on November 30, 1982, has achieved over 104 million sales and is the best-selling album ever. It spent 80 consecutive weeks on the American chart, 37 at number 1, and still sells an estimated 60,000 units in the USA per year.

Jackson has had seven number one singles in the UK:

1981: One Day In Your Life
1983: Billie Jean
1987: I Just Can't Stop Loving You
1991: Black Or White
1995: You Are Not Alone
1995: Earth Song
1997: Blood on the Dance Floor

The English multi-instrumentalist musician and composer **Mike Oldfield** is best known for his groundbreaking 1973 album, Tubular Bells, which launched Virgin Records. He performed the first-ever gig at the National Exhibition Centre in Birmingham.

In November 2006, fellow musician Noel Gallagher won a Spanish court case against Oldfield. The Oasis mastermind had bought an Ibiza villa from the Reading-born performer seven years earlier but quickly discovered that part of the cliff-top property was falling into the sea. Gallagher was awarded a six-figure sum in compensation.

Stock Aitken Waterman terrorised the British music scene from the mid-1980s to the early nineties with their sugary-sweet Europop.

Mike (Stock) was one third of the songwriting triptych. He co-wrote and/or co-produced 16 UK number one records with acts such as Pepsi & Shirlie, Big Fun, Hazell

Dean, Samantha Fox, Mel & Kim, **Pat & Mick**, Kylie Minogue, Roland Rat and Rick Astley.

Bret Michaels (Bret Michael Sychak, b. 1963) is best known for his association with rock band Poison. The lead vocalist – who had a much-publicised fling with Pamela Anderson in 2005 – established a film production company with actor Charlie Sheen.

Michael is a song by Scottish band Franz Ferdinand. The fourth single released from their debut eponymous album, the track is notable for its homoerotic lyrics. By providing three tracks on the CD format, instead of two (in what the band described as a "silly schoolboy error"), the single breached UK chart rules resulting in CD sales not counting towards the chart position.

The song was also included as part of the soundtrack for the PlayStation2 game, Gran Turismo 4.

An ambidextrous virtuoso guitarist, **Michael Angelo Batio** received a Bachelor of Arts in Music Theory and Composition from North-eastern Illinois University.

Listed as one of the top 50 fastest guitarists in the world in *Guitar World Magazine*, he is noted for his 'MAB Over-Under' technique. He flips his hand over and under the neck, approaching the strings from above, then below, instead of from under the neck like other guitar players.

Batio taught Tom Morello (Rage Against the Machine and Audioslave) to play.

Don Ross penned **Michael, Michael, Michael** as a tribute to his friend and major influence, **Michael Hedges**. The fingerstyle acoustic and steel guitar innovator played a wide range of musical styles and was considered a dynamic performer on stage.

He was tragically killed, aged 43, in late 1997 when the car he was driving apparently skidded off a rain-slicked S-curve and down a 120-foot cliff.

The REM lead singer, **Michael Stipe**, once dyed his hair yellow with egg yolk when the band were recording in London in 1985.

In a 2001 *Time* interview, the Georgia-born lyricist described himself as a "queer artist" and revealed that he had been in a relationship with "an amazing man" for three years. In previous interviews, he portrayed himself as "an equal opportunity lech" explaining that he does not define himself as gay, straight, or bisexual.

Born in 1930, the Somerset dairy farmer **Michael Eavis** held the first Glastonbury Festival on his farm in Pilton in 1970. The 1,500 revellers paid a pound each to see headlining act Marc Bolan – who charged £500 for his services and arrived at the site in a velvet-covered limousine – and were all offered free milk.

Poet, musician, and composer – of African, American Indian, Italian and German descent – **Michael Franti** (b. 1966) is front man of the band Spearhead and has also been in Beatnigs (1986-1990) and The Disposable Heroes of Hiphoprisy (1991-1993).

In an anti-poverty protest, Franti decided not to wear his shoes, initially for three days, and never went back. "As I walk through the jungle I'm careful not to break branches and step on growing plants that are coming up and not because I'm so caring, but because it hurts."

Michael Holliday (1924-1963) – real name Norman Alexander Milne – was a popular British singer. Singing in a similar style to Bing Crosby, the Liverpudlian had a string of hits in pre-Beatles UK, including two number one singles; The Story of My Life and Starry Eyed. His music career began by winning an amateur talent contest, 'New Voices of Merseyside', and then, while a Merchant Navy seaman, he entered, and won, a contest at Radio City New York City in 1951. Michael suffered from stage fright and had a mental breakdown in 1961; he committed suicide two years later dying from a suspected drugs overdose in Croydon.

By the age of five, Detroit native **Michael 'Cub' Koda** was a drummer and before he had left high school he had formed his own group, The Del-Tinos.

He is perhaps best known for writing Smokin' In The Boys' Room which he performed with his group Brownsville

Station. The song reached number three in the US Billboard charts in 1974.

On June 30th, 2000, aged 51, he became ill and, although he was recovering from kidney disease, he died the next day.

Michael Hucknall (b. 1960), commonly known as **Mick**, is the lead singer of Simply Red. The Mancunian had hits with Holding Back the Years and Money's Too Tight to Mention in the mid-eighties and is an avid Manchester United fan.

The red-head singer was at the Sex Pistols' first Manchester concert, at the Free Trade Hall in 1976. His father wasn't a fan of his music and apparently told him to become a marine biologist.

Michael 'Mickey' Finn (1947-2003) was apparently hired by Marc Bolan to join T-Rex because of his good looks.

In the early 1970s, Finn's contribution as bongocerro – bongo player – backing vocalist, and, occasionally, bassist, was essential. He often wore a green bowler hat.

MUSICAL MICHAEL SMITHS

Michael Joseph Smith: British saxophonist in the pop band Amen Corner.
Mike Smith: English singer-songwriter, lead singer of The Dave Clark Five.

Mike Smith: British saxophonist, member of the rock band The Ailerons.

≫◆≪

UK PLACES WITH MICHAEL IN THE TITLE

Michael Wood Service Area, Gloucestershire
Michael's Nook, Cumbria
Michaelchurch, Herefordshire
Michaelchurch Court, Herefordshire
Michaelchurch Escley, Herefordshire
Michaelchurch-on-Arrow, Powys
Michaelmuir, Aberdeenshire
Michaelston-le-Pit, Vale of Glamorgan
Michaelston-super-Ely, Cardiff
Michaelston-y-Fedw, Newport
Michaelstow, Cornwall
Michaelstow Ho, Cornwall
Michaelwood Farm, Gloucestershire
Michaelwood Lodge Farm, Gloucestershire
Michaelwood Services, Gloucestershire

Michael (Manx: Mael) is a district and parish in the Isle of Man. Before 1989, it was divided into two local authority areas, **Michael Village Commissioners** and **Michael Parish Commissioners**.

From the west, it stretches from the Irish Sea inland to Druidale to the east, from Orrisdale in the north and to Glen Cam, in the south. The main road between the towns of Peel and Ramsey joins the Isle of Man TT course. The village of **Kirk Michael** is the main centre of population.

THE ROAD TO MICHAEL

There are three **Michael Roads** in London: off Leytonstone Road, E11; a few football pitches away from Selhurst Park – home of Crystal Palace FC – in SE25; and just a few hundred yards away from Chelsea FC's Stamford Bridge in SW6.

There are no **Michael Streets** in England's capital.

MICHAEL – THE FILMS

Michael (1924)

Michael (also known as Mikaël) was a silent film released in 1924. Along with *Different From the Others* (1919) and *Sex in Chains* (1928), *Michael* is widely considered a landmark in gay silent cinema.

The film is based on Herman Bang's 1902 novel *Mikaël* and depicts painter Claude Zoret's love for one of his models, Michael. For a time the two live happily as partners, despite Zoret being considerably older.

As they age, Michael begins to drift from him, although Zoret is completely oblivious to this. A bankrupt countess comes to Zoret for a portrait but plans to seduce him and steal his money. Michael is more receptive to her advances and the two are soon an item. She uses her new lover to steal from Zoret and the painter is left broken when he discovers her dastardly deeds.

Michael sells the painting of himself that Zoret made and gave to him as a gift. He then steals and sells the sketches Zoret made of their time in Algiers, where they first fell in love. The spurned lover then begins work on his masterpiece: a large-scale painting of a man lying on a beach, using the Algerian capital as a background, depicting 'a man who has lost everything'.

Zoret falls ill after finishing the painting. On his deathbed, the visiting Charles Switt – who had always loved Zoret and never criticised Michael as he knew it would upset the painter – beckons Michael to come at once but the Countess prevents him from receiving the message.

Zoret's last words, which also serve as the prologue to the film, are "Now I can die in peace, for I have seen true love."

Michael (1996)

The 1996 version of *Michael*, totally unrelated to the 1924 film, stars John Travolta as the Archangel Michael, who is sent to Earth to undertake various tasks, including mending some wounded hearts.

The American fantasy motion picture, contrary to popular depictions of angels, portrays Michael as a smoking, boozing, oversexed slob – but a character capable of imparting unexpected wisdom. The film cost almost $100m and also featured Andie MacDowell, William Hurt and Bob Hoskins as people who cross Michael's path.

⇒━◆━⇐

ARE YOU TAKING THE MICKEY?

Traditional Cockney rhyming slang works by taking two words that are related through a short phrase and using the first word to stand for a word that rhymes with the second. Popular examples include: apples and pears (stairs), pork pies (lies) and horse and cart (fart).

"Taking the **Mickey**" or "Taking the **Michael**" is an abbreviated form of the Cockney rhyming slang "take the

Mickey Bliss", meaning "take the piss". It first appeared in the 1930s.

Metal Mickey – sickie. "I think he's pulled a Metal Mickey today."
Michael Caine – train or stain.
Michael Winner – dinner.
Mick Jagger – lager.
Mick Mills – pills.
Mickey Duff – puff (marijuana).
Mickey Mouse (1) – house or something that is "rubbish".
"Those trainers are a bit Mickey Mouse, mate."
Mickey Mouse (2) – Scouse (originating from Liverpool).
"He's a Mickey Mouser."
Michael Schumachers – knackers (testicles). Schumacher is German for cobbler.
Michael Miles – piles (haemorrhoids). "Me Michael Miles are playing up."
Mickey Most – toast.

GRANGE HILL MICHAELS

The BBC children's television programme, originally set in a fictional secondary school in North London, achieved cult status in the 1980s with it's Just Say No anti-drugs song, and the portrayal of popular characters including Zammo, Ziggy, Gonch, Tucker, Pogo Patterson and Danny Kendall.

Three **Michaels** have played teachers since the show's 1978 inception.

Michael Percival – Mr Tony Mitchell – was Tucker's form tutor in the very first series.

Michael Cronin – Mr Geoff 'Bullet' Baxter – was a gym teacher from 1979 to 1986.

Michael Sheard – Mr Maurice Bronson – played the fearsome teacher from 1985-1989. The very sight of 'Bronco' would send fear into the pupils, and some of the teachers too. His Hitler-style toupee was glorious ammunition for the cheekier schoolchildren.

≈≻◆≺≈

WHAT DOES MICHAEL MEAN, EXACTLY?
(www.urbandictionary.com)

A dull/common person: someone who is lacking power and is mediocre in influence and potential. Maybe a judgemental person but has no credentials to back up the bravado. This term can be applied to anyone that thinks they are better than they really are yet have nothing to show for it.

USAGE:
1. "He had no idea what the theory of relativity was… he's such a **Michael***."*
2. "He envied Joe because he could always command a crowd. He then realised he was just a **Michael** *and no one took him seriously."*

FUNNY MICHAELS

Michael Chiklis is an Emmy- and Golden Globe-winning American actor and is best known as Ben Grimm/The Thing in the *Fantastic Four* films.

Michael Fenton Stevens was born in 1947; the actor/comedian was the voice behind the *Spitting Image* number one hit in 1986, The Chicken Song.

Michael Patrick King is an Emmy-winning director, writer and producer for television shows including *Sex & the City*, *Will & Grace*, *Cybill*, and *Murphy Brown*.

Michael Legge is an Irish stand-up comedian and television host nominated for a BAFTA award for his writing for MTV.

Illinois-born **Michael John Nelson** is an American comedian and writer, most famous for his work on the cult television series *Mystery Science Theater 3000*. He is married to Bridget Jones.

Michael Edward Palin, CBE was born in Sheffield in 1943. The comedian, actor, writer and television presenter is best known for being one of the members of the comedy group *Monty Python* and appeared in the famous The Dead

Parrot, The Lumberjack Song, The Spanish Inquisition and Spam sketches.

Star of countless TV programmes, films and travel documentaries over forty years, Palin had a small cameo role in Australian soap opera *Home & Away* where he played an English surfer with a fear of sharks.

The part of eccentric Cosmo Kramer on the American television series *Seinfeld* is played by American comedian **Michael Anthony Richards**. Born in 1949, Richards was a scriptwriter on live TV show *ABC Fridays* in the early 80s. Andy Kaufman was the host and during a sketch broke character and refused to read his lines.

Richards threw the cue cards on the table in front of Kaufman, who responded by throwing a glass of water on Richards. The show's cast and crew members then became embroiled in a mini riot on stage.

Mike Yarwood, OBE was one of Britain's top-rated impressionists on television from the mid 1960s to the early 1980s. Before making the nation laugh, he was a salesman at a garment warehouse and almost pursued a career as a professional footballer.

The Stockport-born performer entered The Priory in 1999 to receive treatment for depression.

Michael Ciaran Parker, better known as **Michael Barrymore**, was a prime-time TV constant for much of the 1980s and 90s after winning *New Faces* in 1979.

Managed by wife, Cheryl, the lanky, hyperactive presenter from Essex came out to a packed East End pub in 1995 with the immortal words, "Start spreading the news, I'm gay today".

Born in 1922, **Michael Bentine** CBE was a comedian, comic actor, and member of The Goons. He spoke fluent Spanish and French and volunteered for services in World War II. He was arrested on stage for desertion in 1940, unaware of a RAF conscription notice that had been following him for a month as his company toured.

Before commencement of RAF flight training, he was to be inoculated against typhoid. He was the penultimate man to receive his jab. The vaccine ran out and was mistakenly refilled with a pure culture of typhoid resulting in the death of the other man. Bentine was in a coma for six weeks. The incident left him myopic until his death in 1996.

Michael Patrick Dumbell-Smith is more commonly known as **Michael Crawford**. Famous for his "Ooo Betty" catchphrase in the popular BBC TV sitcom *Some Mothers Do 'Ave 'Em*, the performer decided to change his surname while riding on a bus and spotting a lorry adorned with the slogan 'Crawford's Biscuits Are Best'.

Mike Winters, born Michael Weinstein in 1930, formed a comedy double act with his brother, Bernie, in the 1950s.

In 1955 the duo first appeared on BBC television in a show called *Variety Parade*. They remained with the programme for three years.

Their move to ITV, and the *Sunday Night at the London Palladium*, was organised by their agent Joe Collins (father of Joan and Jackie).

After hosting their own show for years, the act fell apart by 1978 amidst well-publicised animosity between the pair.

Mike emigrated to the United States while Bernie went solo in the UK, forming a successful partnership with a St. Bernard named Schnorbitz.

$$\Longrightarrow\!\!\Longleftarrow$$

INNOVATIVE MICHAELS

Michael Faraday (1791-1867) discovered electro-magnetic induction, electro-magnetic rotations, the magneto-optical effect, diamagnetism and field theory, amongst other things! His picture was printed on British £20 banknotes from 1991 until 2001.

Michel Casseux (1794-1869), a French pharmacist, was a key figure in the shift from street-fighting to the modern sport of savate in France. The martial art uses both the hands and feet as weapons and combines elements of western boxing with graceful kicking techniques. Fighters wear shoes and only foot kicks are allowed. Head-butting, eye gouging and grappling were banned in 1825.

<hr>

RECORD-BREAKING MICHAELS

Mike Holland, the American ski jumper, set the world distance record in 1985 as a 24-year-old. His world record jump of 186 metres – the first man to jump over 600 feet – in Planica, Slovenia held for just 27 minutes before Finnish jumper Matti Nykänen passed his mark with a jump of three metres further.

Michael Watson tragically collapsed at the end of his world super-middleweight defeat to Chris Eubank in 1991. The former boxer spent forty days in a coma, had six brain operations and is still partially paralysed. He bravely completed the London marathon in the slowest ever time – 6 days, 2 hours, 26 minutes and 18 seconds – in 2003.

While Edwin 'Buzz' Aldrin and Neil Armstrong were walking on the moon on July 20th 1969, their colleague **Michael Collins** orbited in the mission's command module.

Michael 'Eddie the Eagle' Edwards became a hero around the world for his 'awful' performance at the 1988 Winter Olympics in Calgary, Canada. The ski-jumper from Cheltenham achieved the British record of 73.5 metres but still finished 58th (last), some 20 metres behind the next worst!

Eddie the Eagle, a film chronicling his life story, went into production in January 2008 with Steve Coogan in the title role. The Eagle is said to be pleased with the casting, although after selling the movie rights in 2001 he thought that either Brad Pitt or Tom Cruise would be best suited for the role.

Mike Melvill – born in South Africa in November 1940 – was the second oldest person in space when he piloted SpaceShipOne on its first flight past the edge of space, flight 15P on June 21, 2004 – thus becoming the first commercial astronaut and the 433rd person to go into space.

Mike Tyson became the youngest heavyweight boxing champion of all time when, aged 20 years and 4 months, he beat Trevor Berbick, by second round Technical Knock Out for the World Boxing Council (WBC) title.

Michael Schumacher is statistically the best Formula One motor racing driver ever. The first billionaire sportsman, the German raced with Jordan, then Benetton for four seasons, winning his first drivers' championship in 1994. Another title followed the next year before a move to Ferrari in 1996. He got back to winning ways in 2000, triumphing in the first of five successive championship victories.

A selection of Schumacher's F1 records:

Championship titles: 7 (1994, 1995, 2000, 2001, 2002, 2003, 2004)
Consecutive titles: 5 (2000–2004)
Race victories: 91
Consecutive wins: 7 (2004, Europe–Hungary)
Wins with one team: 72 (Ferrari)
Wins at same GP: 8 (France)
Wins at different GPs: 22
Longest time between first and last wins: 14 years, 1 month and 2 days
Second places: 43
Podiums (Top 3): 154
Pole positions: 68
Front row starts: 115
Fastest laps: 76

French footballer **Michel Platini** scored a record nine goals at the 1984 Uefa European Championships in his home country.

The midfielder scored an incredible 224 goals in 432 games for AS Nancy, Saint Etienne (both France) and Juventus (Italy), respectively, and is the only player to have been crowned European Footballer of the Year (Ballon d'Or) in three consecutive years, 1983/84/85.

Mike Hailwood, MBE was a British Grand Prix motorcycle road racer regarded by many as one of the greatest racers of all time. Known as 'Mike the Bike', he won four consecutive Fédération Internationale de Motocyclisme (FIM) world championships from 1962 to 1965 and was victorious in 76 races overall.

After an 11-year break from motorcycling, Hailwood triumphed at the Isle of Man TT as a 38-year-old in 1978.

Tragically, in 1981 he was killed along with his daughter Michelle when a lorry made an illegal turn across a central reservation. The lorry driver was fined £100.

Irish dancer **Michael Flatley** set a world record for a tapping speed at 28 taps per second in May 1989, breaking it nine years later with a speed of 35 taps. The current record holder, as at 2008, is namesake **Michael Donnellan**, at 40 taps per second!

ACCIDENTAL MICHAELS

Actor **Michael Massee** fired a stunt pistol at Brandon Lee
– son of Bruce – on the set of *The Crow* in 1993. The tip of
a dummy bullet used in an earlier scene had become lodged
in the gun's chamber and was propelled by a blank straight
at the 28-year-old, killing him instantly.

Michael J. Smith was one of the seven astronauts
that perished on the Challenger shuttle on March 26th
1986. Uttering the words 'uh oh', he was recorded just
before NASA's unblemished safety record was blown to
smithereens after one minute and 14 seconds.

British television and radio presenter **Mike Smith**, a fully
qualified helicopter pilot, famously crashed his vehicle in
1988, breaking his back and ankle. His girlfriend Sarah
Greene – a former *Blue Peter* presenter – smashed both legs
and an arm leaving her unable to have children. The couple
married the following year.

Michael Anderson was a NASA astronaut on the space
shuttle Columbia. The 43-year-old perished when the
STS-107 craft disintegrated on re-entry into the Earth's
atmosphere on February 1st 2003.

Michael Locke (b. 1979), aka Pancho, is a Welsh
professional skateboarder. He is also a member of the four-

strong *Dirty Sanchez* team who perform stunts on various UK TV programmes, and their own eponymous show.

As the shortest of the quartet, he is often picked on by his colleagues, particularly when asleep where japes have included having his head and eyebrows shaved; being spray-painted green and having his clothes ripped up to look like the Incredible Hulk after imbibing excessive amounts of vodka; and having two purple dildos sellotaped to his hands, again, while enjoying some shut-eye.

<hr>

RULING MICHAELS

Russians

Mikhail of Vladimir (1174-1176)
Mikhail Yaroslavich (1304-1318)
Michael I (1613-1645)
Michael II (1917)

Michael of Russia: Mikhail I Feodorovich Romanov (**Michael I**) was the first Russian tsar of the house of Romanov, being the son of Feodor Nikitich Romanov, and his reign marked the end of the Time of Troubles.
He was married twice, first to Princess Maria Vladimirovna Dolgorukova in 1624 – who died four months after the marriage the next year – and then in 1626 to Eudoxia Streshneva (1608-1645), who gave him ten children.

Mikhail Gorbachev was president of the Soviet Union in 1990-91. His efforts to democratise his country's political system and decentralise its economy led to the downfall of communism and the break-up of the Soviet Union in 1991. He was awarded the Nobel Prize for Peace in 1990.

Byzantine emperors

The term 'Byzantine Empire' is used to describe the Greek-speaking Roman Empire of the Middle Ages, centred on its capital of Constantinople (Istanbul, Turkey). A **Michael** reigned for over 500 years.

Michael I (reign): 811-813
Michael II: 820-829
Michael III: 842-867
Michael IV the Paphlagonian: 1034-1041
Michael V: 1041-1042
Michael VI: 1056-1057
Michael VII: 1067-1078
Michael VIII Palaiologos: 1259-1282
Michael IX Palaiologos: 1294/1295-1320

Known as a womaniser and a drunkard – he was rumoured to have over fifty mistresses – Michael Palaeologus (died 1156) was an early member of the great family of the Palaeologi, which later ruled the Byzantine Empire.

King of Poland – **Michał Korybut Wiśniowiecki**: 1669-1673

King of Portugal – **Miguel of Portugal** (often translated as **Michael of Portugal**): 1828-1834

The conservative leaning leader spent the last 34 years of his life in exile after losing the three-year Portuguese war to his brother Pedro.

Rulers of Romania

Michael the Brave: (Prince of Wallachia) (1593-1601), of Transylvania (1599-1600), and of Moldavia (1600). Victorious in the Battle of Călugăreni in 1595, one of the most important battles in the history of medieval Romania, **Michael** led his Wallachian army of 25,000 to victory over the Ottomans who had more 150,000 men in their ranks.

The Order of Michael the Brave is Romania's highest military decoration.

Michael I of Romania: 1927-1930 and 1940-1947. The great-great-grandson of Queen Victoria, and a third cousin of Queen Elizabeth II, he is one of the last surviving heads of state from World War II and was forced to abdicate by the Communists on December 30, 1947.

British Royal Family – **Michaels** of Kent
His Royal Highness Prince Michael of Kent, born in 1942, is the third child of George V's fourth son (Prince George, Duke of Kent) and as such is not expected to

undertake royal and official duties. He does not receive an allowance from the Privy Purse and is a qualified Russian interpreter. He is married to **Princess Michael of Kent** (née Baroness Marie-Christine Agnes Hedwig Ida von Reibnitz), who has published several books on the royal families of Europe.

WHAT DOES MIKE MEAN, EXACTLY?
(www.urbandictionary.com)

Possibly a kind of bowel movement; the kind of golden brown you want your marshmallows to be.

USAGE:
"Hey, check this out."
"Wow, nice Mike."

TOP DOG MICHAELS

Michael Mayr was Chancellor of Austria in the First Austrian Republic from November 1920 to June 1921. Twenty years earlier, he became a Professor of Modern History at the University of Innsbruck.

Michael Pedersen Friis' time in Denmark's hotseat lasted from April 5th 1920 to May 5th; just one month. A week earlier King Christian X had dismissed Prime

Minister Carl Theodor Zahle and replaced him with Otto Liebe, but this use of power by the monarch triggered the Easter Crisis of 1920, and Liebe resigned 5 days later. Friis was then appointed head of a caretaker cabinet to lead Denmark until elections could be held and a new government appointed.

A member of the Bubi ethnic group, **Miguel Abia Biteo Boricó** was Equatorial Guinea's prime minister from 2004 to 2006 and is one of the few members of his ethnic group to achieve political power in his country, which is politically dominated by the Fang group.

Considered the 'father' of the current Constitution of France, **Michel Debré** became the first Prime Minister of the Fifth Republic – and 150th Prime Minister of France – in 1959.

Born in 1857, **Georg Michaelis** was the first Chancellor of Germany of non-noble background. His reign lasted from July 14th to October 31st in 1917.

Writer of seven books, including the award-winning *A History of West Indies Cricket*, **Michael Manley** of the People's National Party enjoyed two terms as Jamaica prime minister: 1972-1980 and 1989-1992.

A miner before becoming a Labour politician, **Michael Savage** – regarded by many as his country's greatest leader – served as Prime Minister of New Zealand from 1935 and died in office five years later, aged 68.

Sir Michael Thomas Somare has been Prime Minister of Papua New Guinea on three occasions; from independence in 1975 until 1980, again from 1982 until 1985 (both as a member of the Pangu Party), and since the 2002 election as leader of the National Alliance Party.

Relations with Australia became strained when he refused to remove his shoes at Brisbane Airport resulting in a diplomatic contretemps and a protest march on the Australian High Commission, demanding an apology, in Port Moresby.

Mick Collins (1890-1922) was an Irish revolutionary leader, Director of Intelligence for the IRA, and member of the Irish delegation during the Anglo-Irish Treaty negotiations. In 1917, he was elected to the Sinn Fein executive, creating an intelligence network, organising a national loan to fund a rebellion and assembling an assassination squad ('The Twelve Apostles') and an arms-smuggling operation.

By 1920, he was wanted by the British and had a £10,000 price on his head. He was shot and killed in August 1922, during an ambush in the Irish Civil War. He never learned to swim and his father, **Michael John Collins**, was 75 years old when his youngest son was born.

Michael L. Eskew was chairman of UPS (United Parcel Service) – the company has designed and trademarked its own font, UPS Sans, for use in marketing and communication material – from 2002 to 2007 and now sits on the board at 3M and IBM.

Michael Dammann Eisner (b. 1942) was CEO of The Walt Disney Company from September 22nd 1984 to September 30th 2005 and also narrated all Disney previews during that time.

Prince Michael Andreas Barclay de Tolly (1761-1818) – born in Lithuania but a member of the Scottish Clan Barclay – was a Russian Field Marshal and Minister of War during Napoleon's invasion of Russia.

Barclay served against the Turks, Swedes and Poles, became a colonel in 1798 and a major-general in 1799. In the war of 1806 against Napoleon, he fought in the Battle of Pultusk and was wounded at the Battle of Eylau (February 7th 1807).

Immortalised by the Russian poet Baratynsky for leading the battle to seize Umeå in Sweden in 1809, he was made Governor-General of Finland. He successfully drove Bonaparte and his men out of Russia in 1812.

Born in Damascus, Syria to a middle-class Greek Orthodox Christian family, **Michel Aflaq** (1910, died 1989) was the founder of Ba'athism, a form of secular Arab nationalism.

Michael Rosen (b. 1946) succeeded Jacqueline Wilson as the fifth Children's Laureate in June 2007. The broadcaster, children's novelist, poet, and author of 140 books, once presented a 1970s series on BBC Schools television called *WALRUS* (**W**rite **A**nd **L**earn, **R**ead, **U**nderstand, **S**peak).

⟞⬦⟝

FAILING MICHAELS

Nominated for 'best actor' Oscar
(real Michaels)

1947 – **Michael Redgrave**:
Mourning Becomes Electra as 'Orin Mannon'

1966 – **Michael Caine**:
Alfie as 'Alfie'

1972 – **Michael Caine**:
Sleuth as 'Milo Tindle'

1983 – **Michael Caine**:
Educating Rita as 'Dr. Frank Bryant'

2002 – **Michael Caine**:
The Quiet American as 'Thomas Fowler'

Nominated for 'best actor' Oscars
(Michael characters)

1949 – Kirk Douglas:
Champion as '**Michael 'Midge' Kelly**'

1974 – Al Pacino:
The Godfather, Part II as '**Michael Corleone**'

1978 – Robert De Niro:
The Deer Hunter as '**Michael Vronsky**'

1981 – Paul Newman:
Absence of Malice as '**Michael Colin Gallagher**'

1982 – Dustin Hoffman:
Tootsie as '**Michael Dorsey/Dorothy Michaels**'

2007 – George Clooney:
Michael Clayton as '**Michael Clayton**'

Nominated for 'best supporting actor' Oscars
(real Michaels)

1945 – **Michael Chekhov**:
Spellbound as 'Dr. Alexander 'Alex' Brulov'

1965 – **Michael Dunn**:
Ship of Fools as 'Carl Glocken'

1967 – **Michael J. Pollard**:
Bonnie and Clyde as 'C.W. Moss'

1974 – **Michael V. Gazzo**:
The Godfather Part II as 'Frankie Pentangeli'

1980 – **Michael O'Keefe**:
The Great Santini as 'Ben Meechum'

1991 – **Michael Lerner**:
Barton Fink as 'Jack Lipnick'

1999 – **Michael Clarke Duncan**:
The Green Mile as 'John Coffey'

Nominated for 'best supporting actor' Oscars
(Michael characters)

1972 – Al Pacino:
The Godfather as '**Michael Corleone**'

2007 – Tom Wilkinson:
Michael Clayton as 'Arthur Edens'

WINNING MICHAELS

Oscar-winning best actor Michael

1987 – **Michael Douglas**:
Wall Street as 'Gordon Gekko'

Oscar-winning best supporting actor Michaels

1970 – John Mills:
Ryan's Daughter as '**Michael**'

1986 – **Michael Caine**:
Hannah and Her Sisters as 'Elliot'

1999 – **Michael Caine**:
The Cider House Rules as 'Dr. Wilbur Larch'

OLYMPIC MICHAELS

Over a period of eight years, **Michael Johnson** dominated 400 metres in men's athletics and is the only sprinter in history to win both the 200m and 400m at the same Olympics, accomplishing the feat at the 1996 Summer Olympics in Atlanta. He is also the only man to successfully defend his 400m title.

The Dallas-born (1967) athlete was nicknamed the 'Duck' for his unique running style; upright stance with very short steps characterised by his head bobbing backwards and forwards, straightness of his back and not much arm drive.

Gold 1992 – Barcelona: 4 x 400m relay
Gold 1996 – Atlanta: 200m
Gold 1996 – Atlanta: 400m
Gold 2000 – Sydney: 400m
Gold 2000 – Sydney: 4 x 400m relay

Michael 'The Albatross' Gross won three Olympic gold medals in the 1980s. Standing at 6ft 7 ins., and with a total span of 2.27 metres, Gross represented West Germany in two Games.

1984 Los Angeles – Gold: 200m Freestyle
1984 Los Angeles – Gold: 100m Butterfly
1988 Seoul – Gold: 200m Butterfly

Michael Greis is a German biathlete. The Bavarian won three gold medals at the Turin Winter Olympics in 2006; 20 km individual, 4 x 7.5km relay and the 15km mass start.

Mike Burton's swimming career began when, at the age of 13, he was hit head-on by a truck while cycling. After eight weeks in hospital with a dislocated hip and torn ligaments in his right leg, he was told that swimming was the only sport he could pursue.

He won two gold medals at the 1968 Mexico City Olympics including the 1,500m by a record margin of 18.4 seconds. He defended his title at the distance four years later in Munich.

Beijing 2008 Olympic medallists

Named World Swimmer of the Year four times in 2003, 2004, 2006 and 2007, **Michael Fred Phelps II** won an incredible eight gold medals:

Distance	**Time** (in mins and secs)
400m individual medley	4:03.84
4 x 100m freestyle relay	3:08.24
200m freestyle	1:42.96
200m butterfly	1:52.03

4 x 200m freestyle relay	6:58.56
200m individual medley	1:54.23
100m butterfly	0:50.58
4 x 100m medley relay	3:29.34

Other medallists…

Gold
Men's 4 x 100m relay: **Michael Frater** (Jamaica)
Men's basketball: **Michael Redd** (USA)
Men's slalom C-1 canoeing: **Michal Martikán** (Slovakia)
Men's handball: **Michaël Guigou** (France)
Men's rowing (quadruple sculls): **Michal Jelinski** (Poland)

Silver
Men's 4 x 400m relay: **Michael Mathieu** (Bahamas)
Men's baseball: **Michel Enríquez** (Cuba)
Men's K-4 1000m flatwater canoeing: **Michal Riszdorfer** (Slovakia)
Men's team pursuit cycling (track) : **Michael Mørkøv** (Denmark) and **Michael Færk Christensen** (Denmark)
Men's inaugural BMX: **Mike Day** (USA)

Bronze
Men's baseball: **Michael Koplove** (USA) and **Mike Hessman** (USA)
Men's lightweight coxless four: **Mike Lewis** (USA)
Men's tennis (doubles): **Mike Bryan** (with twin brother Bob) USA

VERY STUPID MICHAELS

Bum note

Alcoholic Texan **Michael** was addicted to enemas.
Most people stop drinking, or pass out, when they've had
enough... not this particularly stupid Michael. One night
the 56-year-old decided to imbibe three litres of sherry
through his anus, with help from his loyal wife Tammy Jean.

After a mammoth 'drinking' session he passed out, with
the remaining sherry fermenting in his rectal cavity.
Needless to say, he did not surface the next day. Toxicology
reports measured his blood alcohol level as 0.47%. He had
effectively embalmed himself!

For his achievements, Michael earned a 2007 Darwin Award.

Nitro Mike

A group of physics students held their annual welcome back
party. **Michael**, the class boffin, impressed his peers with
tales of drinking liquid nitrogen, without injury, several
years earlier in a cryogenics lab.

Naturally, his fellow party-goers were somewhat sceptical.
"It will freeze your whole body. Remember Terminator 2?"
was one concerned, if not mocking, response.

He was confident. He downed a shot assuming he would
blow smoke out his nose and impress everyone. Within two

seconds, Mike had collapsed, unable to breathe or indeed do anything except feel intense pain.

Unsurprisingly, you should not drink liquid nitrogen. It can be safely held in your mouth for blowing smoke patterns. It should never, ever, ever be swallowed. The closed epiglottis prevents the gas from escaping, so expanding gas is forced into the body.

Nitro Mike, as he was thereafter christened, was badly burned from epiglottis to the stomach bottom, suffered a collapsed lung and was in theatre for all-night surgery.

He is the first documented medical case of a cryogenic ingestion.

Mike the missile

According to urban legend, a group of young men were drinking beer and shooting guns in the rear garden of **Irving Michaels**' house in Carbon County, Pennsylvania in 1998.

They were firing at a raccoon but the alcohol perhaps impaired their aim as, despite an estimated 35 shots, the animal escaped into a three-inch diameter drainage pipe, 100 feet away.

Not to be outdone, Michaels poured 15 litres of petrol down the pipe, intending to smoke the animal out.

After several unsuccessful attempts to ignite the fuel, he proceeded to slide feet-first approximately 15 feet down the sloping pipe to toss the match.

The resulting fireball jettisoned Michaels – "like a Polaris missile leaves a submarine," according to a witness – over his home, right over the heads of his stunned friends, and onto his front lawn. A total distance of 200 feet!

What does Michael mean, exactly?

(www.urbandictionary.com)

Michael is a term for a man who pretends to be a woman in order to pick up gay men online.

USAGE:

*"He went online and pretended to be a **Michael** to pick up gay men. You should have seen the smile on his face."*

<hr>

Ig Nobel Prize winners

The Ig Nobel Prizes honour achievements that first make people laugh, and then make them think.

In 2004 **Michael Tyler** of the University of Adelaide was awarded for painstakingly smelling and cataloguing the peculiar odours produced by 131 different species of frogs when the amphibians were feeling stressed.

In the same year, **Michael Turvey**, of the University of Connecticut and Haskins Laboratory, received a deserved accolade for exploring and explaining the dynamics of hula-hooping.

The year 2003 was pivotal for Physics as **Michael Lawrance** and a team of Australian scientists produced a crucial report entitled 'An Analysis of the Forces Required to Drag Sheep over Various Surfaces'.

Sir Michael Berry of Bristol University teamed up
with Andre Geim of the University of Nijmegen (the
Netherlands) to levitate a frog using magnets.

In Medicine, Marcia E. Buebel, David S. Shannahoff-
Khalsa, and **Michael R. Boyle** conducted an invigorating
study entitled 'The Effects of Unilateral Forced Nostril
Breathing on Cognition'.

<hr>

UNDISPUTED MICHAELS

Brother of heavyweight champion Leon Spinks, **Michael**
was undisputed light-heavyweight champion of the world
between March 18th, 1983 and September 21st, 1985. He
was the first world light heavyweight champion to win the
world heavyweight title, beating Larry Holmes in 1986, thus
making Michael and Leon the first brothers to be world
heavyweight champions.

Born a month before England won the FIFA World Cup in
1966, **Mike Tyson** was undisputed heavyweight boxing
champion of the world for 925 days.

<u>1987</u>
August 1 – Tony Tucker, Las Vegas – W (round) 12
(Won IBF Heavyweight Title. Retained WBA/WBC Heavyweight Titles.
Became Undisputed World Heavyweight Champion)
October 16 – Tyrell Biggs, Atlantic City, New Jersey –
Technical Knock Out 7
(Retained Undisputed World Heavyweight Title)

<u>1988</u>
January 22 – Larry Holmes, Atlantic City, New Jersey – TKO 4
(Ret. Undisputed World Heavyweight Title)
March 21 – Tony Tubbs, Tokyo, Japan – TKO 2
(Ret. Undisputed World Heavyweight Title)
June 27 – Michael Spinks, Atlantic City, New Jersey – KO 1
(Ret. Undisputed World Heavyweight Title)

<u>1989</u>
February 25 – Frank Bruno, Las Vegas – TKO 5
(Ret. Undisputed World Heavyweight Title)
July 21 – Carl Williams, Atlantic City, New Jersey – TKO 1
(Ret. Undisputed World Heavyweight Title)

<u>1990</u>
February 11 – James Douglas, Tokyo, Japan – KO by 10
(Lost World Heavyweight Title)

Michael Jordan is widely regarded as the best basketball player of all time. The 6ft 6ins. Brooklyn-born shooting guard graduated from the University of North Carolina in 1984, aged 21, and joined Chicago Bulls.

In 1991, he won his first NBA championship, which was followed with further titles in 1992 and 1993. Jordan abruptly left the NBA in October 1993 to pursue a career in baseball with the Chicago White Sox but rejoined the Bulls in 1995, leading them to three successive championships from 1996.

Jordan retired for a second time in 1999, but returned for two more NBA seasons with Washington Wizards. He holds over 200 records as a Chicago Bull and scored over ten points in all but one of his 1,109 games for the Illinois side; 8 points on March 25, 1986 versus the Cleveland Cavaliers.

MICHAELS IN THE SQUARE

E8 was a working title for the London-based soap opera EastEnders. Ridley Road Market in Dalston, a short pedestrianised road that features a daily market and established street vendors, is 'closest' to the real Albert Square.

Michael Pariss (1990) – played by Matthew Line

Arriving in 1996, **Michael Rose** – played by Russell Floyd – was a market inspector whose ex-wife, Susan, was suffering from multiple sclerosis. He ended up caring for her, they got back together, he then had an affair with Lisa, who would eventually have a child with Phil Mitchell. His son Matthew was wrongly imprisoned for the murder of Saskia Duncan.

Michael Nee was a young trainee taxi driver, Christopher Fry, who appeared on 3rd February, 2004 expressing an interest in buying Charlie Slater's vehicle.

Michael Rawlins lasted for five weeks in 2005 as a driving instructor who taught Dot Branning, nee Cotton, how to drive. The character was played by Melvyn Hayes, who is best known for playing the effeminate Gunner (later Bombardier) 'Gloria' Beaumont in the BBC sitcom *It Ain't Half Hot Mum*.

Michael Higgs played The Firm boss, Andy Hunter, from 2003 to 2005. He was due to marry Kat Slater but Alfie Moon gatecrashed their wedding day to declare his undying love for the barmaid.

Hunter was owed a large sum of money by Moon and blackmailed Kat to have sex with him in order to pay off the debt. If she had refused, he would have Alfie killed.

Hunter then married Sam Mitchell and persuaded her to sign over her house. He was pushed off a motorway bridge in 2004 and Mitchell, expecting to inherit everything, was shocked to discover this immortal line in his will: "To my wife, I leave her the engagement ring so she can sell it, get her roots done, and still be the dumbest blonde I had ever known."

Michael Begley   last appeared as PC Jim Sellers in 2003
Michael Conrad   last appeared as Ray Pinner in 2003
Michael Greco   last appeared as Beppe di Marco in 2002
Michael Jayston   last appeared as Alistair Wilson in 2001
Michael Elphick   last appeared as Harry Slater in 2001
Michael Fenner   last appeared as David Walker in 2001

The Reverend Adam Cherry, played by **Michael Fenton Stevens**, was the vicar who conducted Ethel Skinner's funeral in September 2000.

Willy Roper, dubbed 'Wicked Willy' by the British press and played by **Michael Tudor-Barnes**, framed Arthur Fowler for embezzlement in 1996, leading to his wrongful imprisonment.

Michael French played David Wicks for three years until 1996. The character will be best remembered for almost having sex with his daughter, Bianca.

Michael Roberts last appeared as Harry Samson in 1993.

Michael Melia's character, Eddie Royle, landlord of the Queen Victoria, was stabbed to death by Nick Cotton in 1991.

Colin Russell was the soap opera's first openly gay character in 1986 and left three years later. Actor **Michael Cashman** (b. 1950) was born three weeks prematurely, partially due to his mother defending his father in a street fight.

MICHAELS ON THE STREET

The working title for the longest-running soap opera in the world was *Florizel Street*. A tea lady named Agnes suggested the name sounded like a brand of disinfectant so the name was changed. Relatively few Michaels – both characters and actors – have appeared in the fictional setting of Weatherfield since it was first broadcast in 1960.

Michael Vernon 'Mike' Baldwin – Johnny Briggs

One of the longest-running characters, Baldwin first appeared on our TV screens on Monday 11th October 1976.

The Cockney wide-boy was married four times, and had 25 girlfriends, including Deirdre – whose 1981 wedding to longstanding rival Ken Barlow was watched by over 24 million viewers, a higher figure than for the wedding of the Prince of Wales to Lady Diana Spencer in the same year – Susan Barlow (Ken's daughter), Alma Sedgewick and Jackie Ingram, whom he married for a week before she held a gun to his head asking him to leave.

The character was diagnosed with Alzheimer's Disease in 2005 and died in the arms of arch-nemesis Ken, on Friday 7th April 2006, uttering the immortal line: "You're finished Barlow, Deirdre loves me, she's mine."

Michael Jayston played the Judge (2000) at Jim McDonald's sentencing.

Michael Le Vell (real name **Michael Turner**) has played mechanic Kevin Webster since 1983.

Michael Starke – who played Sinbad for 16 years in the long-running soap *Brookside* – portrays kebab shop owner Jerry Morton on the cobbles. He shares his name with Michael J. Starke, an American classical music composer and period instrumentalist who composes choral music for church services broadcast over Armed Forces Radio in Japan.

David Michaels played hairdresser Jon Welch in 1994. The Mancunian was set to return as a regular character in February 1996 by buying Denise Osbourne's salon. Unfortunately, he badly broke his leg playing football for a National Theatre team resulting in a two-month stay in St. Thomas's Hospital in London, necessitating a major script re-write.

Michael Dixon played Christopher Pitcher in 2006.

⇒◆⇐

ENGLISH FOOTBALLING MICHAELS

Michael Mackay (b. 1982) scored a remarkable 43 goals in half a season for Consett before signing for Hartlepool United in February 2007.

Michael Appleton (b. 1975) retired as a midfielder after a posterior knee ligament injury cut his career short at West Bromwich Albion, aged just 27.

On May 26th, 1989, **Michael Thomas** etched his name in football folklore. His Arsenal side needed to win by two clear goals against Liverpool at Anfield in order to win the First Division title. In injury time, Thomas surged forward from midfield to shoot low past the advancing Bruce Grobbelaar to score Arsenal's second, and secure the London club's first championship in 18 years.

Michael Ball (b. 1979) is a left-back who has played for Everton, Rangers, PSV Eindhoven and Manchester City.

Striker **Mike Flanagan** was a prolific goalscorer for Charlton Athletic – where he was once sent off for fighting with his own team-mate, Derek Hales – and Queens Park Rangers before a stint with the New England Tea Men in the North American Soccer League in 1978.

Midfielder **Michael Johnson** (b. 1988) has represented England at under-19 level and began his career at Everton. While at Manchester City, the youngster has attracted attention from Liverpool, Arsenal, Tottenham Hotspur and Everton.

Right-back **Michael Barron** (b. 1974) played over 300 games for Hartlepool United and arrived late for his testimonial dinner – where Bobby Robson was a guest speaker – as he was playing in a reserve team match.

England midfielder **Michael Carrick** (b. 1981) started life as a centre-forward in his native Newcastle before signing for West Ham United, Tottenham Hotspur and Manchester United. He got married on the same day as international colleagues Steven Gerrard and Gary Neville on 16 June 2007.

Centre-back **Michael Dawson** (b. 1983), formerly of Nottingham Forest, has two brothers that play professional football: Andy (Hull City) and Kevin (ex-Chesterfield).

Defender **Michael Felgate** (b. 1991) plays for Enosis Neon Paralimni in the League Marfin Laiki (the Cypriot Championship First Division).

Midfielder **Mike Bailey** (b. 1942) spent the majority of his playing career with Charlton Athletic and Wolverhampton Wanderers and also represented England twice.

Forward **Michael Elwiss** (b. 1954) played for his local club Doncaster Rovers, Preston North End – where he was named the club's Player of the Year, twice – and Crystal Palace.

Mike Fillery (b. 1960) played in midfield for Chelsea and Queens Park Rangers in the 1970s and 1980s after earning England schoolboy and youth honours.

Despite being born in England, **Michael Johnson** represented Jamaica at international level. He began his career at Notts County in 1991 and went on to play for Birmingham City and Derby County. His nickname was 'Magic' due to his incredible leap.

Michael McNeil (b. 1940) made nine left-back appearances for England in 1960 and 1961.

Michael Maidens (May 7th 1987-October 19th 2007) was a midfielder with Hartlepool United. The youngster tragically lost his life in a car crash.

MASS-MURDERING MICHAELS

Michael McGray has killed at least four people (and claims to have murdered 16) across North America. The Canadian serial killer was charged with the murder of a hitchhiker, whose body had been found 16 years earlier on the side of a road near Digby, Nova Scotia, in May 2001. The victim, 17-year-old Elizabeth Gale Tucker, was murdered while hitchhiking to her job at a fish plant. The killer has stated that he will murder prisoners, guards, or anybody else, to quench a "searing hunger to kill".

Originally from Italy, **Michael Lupo** was a serial killer who carried out attacks in the UK. He ran a flower shop in Chelsea and called himself 'The Wolf Man' and boasted of having 4,000 gay lovers.

Lupo pleaded guilty to four murders – and two attempted killings – at the Old Bailey in 1987. He died from an AIDS related illness in February 1995 and claimed that discovering he had the disease triggered his murderous spree.

Unemployed labourer, **Michael Ryan**, shot and killed sixteen people, including his mother, and wounded 15 others on August 19th August 1987.

The 27-year-old's actions, dubbed The Hungerford massacre, may have been thwarted sooner but the Thames Valley firearms squad were training 40 miles away and the police helicopter was in for repair, though it was eventually deployed.

Michael Ross was executed by lethal injection in 2005 – aged 45 – the first in New England since 1960.
He came from a dysfunctional family, was frequently battered by his mother, and committed the first of eight murders in 1981.

In 1983, nurses at Ohio State University began noticing that apparently healthy patients on floors where **Michael Swango** worked began mysteriously dying with an alarming frequency.

He returned to Illinois and paramedics soon spotted that whenever Swango prepared the coffee or brought any food in, several of them usually became violently ill, with no apparent cause. Arsenic was discovered and he was sentenced to five years' imprisonment. On his 1991 release, Swango forged several legal documents and re-established himself at the Northport Veterans Administration Medical Center in New York.

Once again his patients began dying for no apparent reason. He was dismissed and over 125 medical schools, and over one thousand teaching hospitals, across the States were warned.

Swango resurfaced in Zimbabwe in November 1994. Again, his patients began dying mysteriously. He was arrested and charged with the poisonings but fled before his trial and hid out elsewhere in Africa and Europe before ending up at The Royal Hospital in Dharan, Saudi Arabia a year and half later.

He was finally tried for the murders he had committed in his medical practices on July 11, 2000 and pleaded guilty to killing three of his patients. It is estimated that, over the course of his killing spree, Swango killed anywhere between 30 and 60 people.

Michel Fourniret, the 'Ogre of the Ardennes', is a French serial killer who confessed, in 2004, to kidnapping and murdering nine girls in a span of 14 years during the 1980s and the 1990s.

Writers

Michael Bond, OBE, is an English children's author and the creator of *Paddington Bear*. His other credits include the adventures of a guinea pig named Olga da Polga, the animated BBC TV series *The Herbs*, and *Monsieur Pamplemousse*, culinary mystery stories for adults.

Michael Chabon's first novel, *The Mysteries of Pittsburgh*, was written as his master's thesis in 1988. His professor, Donald Heiney, sent it to a literary agent without Chabon's knowledge, and got the author an impressive $155,000 advance; most first-time novelists receive advances ranging from $5,000 to $7,500.

Michael Collins is the most well-known pseudonym of Dennis Lynds, the American author who died in 2005, aged 81. He published 80 novels and 200 short stories, in both mystery and literary themes, in over four decades.

He penned the *Dan Fortune* stories, one of the longest-running private detective series ever written, from 1967 to 1995.

Odds On, (1966), *The Andromeda Strain* (1969), *The Terminal Man* (1972), *Jurassic Park* (1990), *Disclosure* (1994) and *Next* (2006) are just a handful of **Michael Crichton**'s novels.

Standing at 6ft 9ins. tall, the Chicago-born author – whose work is predominantly in the action genre and heavily features technology – has sold over 150 million books worldwide.

Compiled by **Michael Gerber**, the *Barry Trotter* series – million-selling parodies of the *Harry Potter* books – includes phrases, objects and characters such as;

- Blast-Ended Brewt: disgusting creatures that light their own farts.
- Philosopher's Scone: a mystical baked good which imbues the eater with eternal life.
- Madame Sprig: Hogwash's perpetually-stoned Herbology professor. She used to be a roadie for Bob Marley and the Wailers but they fired her for smoking too much marijuana.

Michael Kenyon (1931-2005) wrote over twenty humorous mystery novels. He was a pioneer in the genre of spoof-espionage story telling and published his first novel, *May You Die In Ireland* in 1967.

Born in Sri Lanka in 1943, **Michael Ondaatje**'s most famous work is *The English Patient*, a 1992 novel adapted into an award-winning film of the same name in 1996.

Michael Shaara (1928-1988) began selling science fiction stories to fiction magazines in the 1950s. An amateur boxer and police officer, he suffered a heart attack aged 36 but fully recovered. His novel about the Battle of Gettysburg, *The Killer Angels*, won the Pulitzer Prize for Fiction in 1975.

Best known for his *Star Wars* and *Battletech* books, **Michael Stackpole** once worked as a designer of role-playing games around the time that accusations flew regarding 'occult' elements of *Dungeons & Dragons* that were allegedly driving people to Satanism, murder and suicide.

Poet **Mick Imlah** passed away, aged 52, in January 2009. His second volume of poetry, *The Lost Leader*, won the 2008 Forward prize for best collection and was shortlisted for the TS Eliot prize.

Imlah, who was diagnosed with motor neurone disease in December 2007, published his first work, *Birthmarks*, in 1988 to critical acclaim.

He was born and raised near Glasgow and combined his highly successful poetry with a parallel career in literary journalism. He was editor of the prestigious *Poetry Review* from 1983 until 1986, and worked at the *Times Literary Supplement* from 1992, where he was poetry editor.

Imlah was described by *The Times'* Neil Corcoran as "a poet of striking originality and cunning, a genuinely distinctive voice in the murmur and babble of the contemporary".

"When I tell people I've slept with more than 130 women, they are appalled but, you know, I've been doing it for 55 years so I don't think that's bad going!"
Michael Winner

POLITICAL MICHAELS

There has never been a British Prime Minister with the first name Michael.

Sir Michael Hicks Beach, the 1st Earl St Aldwyn (1837-1916), was an English statesman. He was Irish Secretary in Lord Salisbury's Cabinet and was replaced by Lord Randolph Churchill, Winston's father, as Conservative Leader of the Commons in 1886.

Michael Denzil Xavier Portillo (b. 1953, in Bushey, Hertfordshire) is a former Conservative Party politician and Cabinet Minister.

His father was an exiled Spanish republican, Luis Gabriel Portillo. He starred in a television commercial for Ribena at the age of eight and now regularly appears on British screens alongside Labour MP Diane Abbott on BBC programme *This Week*.

Michael Mackintosh Foot, who was born in 1913 in Plymouth, Devon. He was made editor of the *Evening Standard* in 1942 at the age of 28. He was leader of the Labour Party from 1980 to the 1983 General Election when his manifesto pledged that a Labour government would abolish the House of Lords, nationalise banks and leave the EEC.

Throughout his political career he railed against the increasing corporate domination of the press, entertaining a special loathing for Rupert Murdoch. He has been a passionate supporter of Plymouth Argyle Football Club since an early age and, as a present for his 90th birthday in 2003, the club registered him as a player and gave him the shirt number, 90. This made him the oldest registered player in the history of football. He has stated that he would not 'conk out' until he had seen his team play in the Premier League.

LABOUR POLITICIANS: CONSTITUENCY/POSITION
(as at March 2009)

Michael Clapham: Barnsley West and Penistone, 1992-onwards

Michael Connarty: Falkirk East, 1992-2005; Linlithgow and Falkirk East, 2005-onwards

Michael Jabez Foster: Hastings and Rye, 1997-onwards

Michael John Foster: Worcester, 1997-onwards

Mike Gapes: Ilford South, 1992-onwards

Mike Hall: Weaver Vale, Cheshire, 1997-onwards

Michael Martin: Glasgow Springburn, 1979-2000

Michael Meacher: Oldham West, 1970-97; Oldham West and Royton, 1997-onwards

Alun Michael: Cardiff South and Penarth, 1987-onwards

Mike O'Brien, North Warwickshire, 1992-onwards

Michael Wills: Swindon North, 1997-onwards

Mike Wood: Batley and Spen, 1997-onwards

CONSERVATIVE POLITICIANS: CONSTITUENCY/ POSITION
(as at March 2009)

Michael Ancram: Berwick and East Lothian, Feb 1974-Oct 1974; Edinburgh South, 1979-1987; Devizes, 1992-onwards

Michael Fabricant: Mid Staffordshire, 1992-1997; Lichfield, 1997-onwards

Michael Fallon: Darlington 1983-1992; Sevenoaks 1997-onwards

Michael Gove: Surrey Heath, 2005-onwards; Shadow Secretary of State for Children, Schools and Families, 2007-onwards

Michael Jack: Fylde, 1987-onwards

Michael Lord: Central Suffolk and North Ipswich, 1983-onwards

Mike Penning: Hemel Hempstead, 2005-onwards

Michael Spicer: South Worcestershire, 1974-1997; West Worcestershire 1997-onwards; Chairman of the 1922 Committee, 2001-onwards

≈≫◆≪≈

WHAT NOT TO CALL YOUR BABY

Mike Hunt
Mike Crotch

WHAT DOES MICHAEL MEAN, EXACTLY?

(www.urbandictionary.com)

A high-speed, head-on collision between two road vehicles, as featured in the NZLTSA (New Zealand Land Transport Safety Authority) safety commercial of the same title that aired in the late 1990s, is referred to as a **Michael** in the land of the White Cloud.

To be a true **Michael** one vehicle must come to rest on its roof after the collision. This definition was met with anger by many crash victims whose accidents they felt were completely deserving of the term, but not technically or officially classified as **Michaels**.

USAGE
1. *"That's not funny, my uncle died in a **Michael**."*
2. *"Drive safe, don't want you getting in to a **Michael** do we?"*

TV PRESENTERS

Mike Morris began life at TV-am as a sports reporter in 1983. Four years later he shuffled alongside Anne Diamond on the sofa to become the show's main presenter.

Michael Aspel has been a regular face on British TV screens since the 1960s. Born in 1933, he was once married to Elizabeth Power – who played Arthur Fowler's mistress, Mrs Hewitt, in *EastEnders* in the early Nineties – and hosted classics such as *Crackerjack*, *This is Your Life* and *Antiques Roadshow*. He announced his retirement in 2007.

Born in 1980, **Michael Gibson** is one of the youngest people ever to be diagnosed with Parkinson's disease. He presented on MTV and made a documentary about his condition, *All Shook Up: Parkinson's at 25*, for Channel Four.

Vic Reeves was best man at the wedding of *Bargain Hunt*'s **Michael Hogben**.

The antiques dealer opened fashion boutique **Mickey Finn** at the age of 17 and ran his own auction house in Folkestone for 15 years until 2004.

Michael Parkinson did National Service as Britain's youngest army captain, and was involved in the Suez Operation (October 1956 to March 1957), before finding fame as a chat show host.

The Kenny Everett character Cupid Stunt was 'interviewed' by a cardboard cut-out of Parkinson in all of 'her' sketches. The Yorkshireman is also one of the figures on the cover of the Wings album Band on the Run.

Michaela Strachan broke many a schoolboys' heart in the 1980s and 90s. As a youthful Saturday morning children's TV presenter, she woke up the nation on TV-am and the *Wide Awake Club*, then joined clubbers across England on the *Hitman & Her* with Pete Waterman before moving on to front *The Really Wild Show* in 1993. She had a brief music career as Michaela with two singles; a cover of H.A.P.P.Y. Radio and Take Good Care Of My Heart.

BBC newsreader **Michael Buerk** famously reported the Ethiopian famine in October 1984, inspiring the Band Aid charity record by Midge Ure and Bob Geldof.

Michael Collie presents BBC *Midlands Today* from Birmingham and has worked in broadcasting since 1986. He has appeared on *Countryfile* and *Top Gear* and has stated that it is his ambition to own a Cadillac hearse.

Mike Bongiorno (b. 1924) is one of the best known hosts on Italian television, famous as il Re del Quiz, 'The Quiz King'.

During World War II he abandoned his studies in Turin, joined a group of Italian partisans, was captured and spent seven months in the San Vittore prison in Milan, before being deported to a German concentration camp. Bongiorno returned to Italy in 1953 and appeared in *Arrivi e Partenze* (Arrivals and Departures) on the very first day of official public TV transmissions in Italy. From 1955 to 1959 he hosted the quiz show *Lascia o Raddoppia?* (Double or Nothing?), the Italian version of *The $64,000 Question*, and became a household name.

Another successful show was *Campanile Sera* (Bell Tower Evening, 1959-1962) where a southern Italian town, and a northern one, challenged each other with a series of questions.

Quiz programme *Rischiatutto* (Risk It All, 1970-1974), the Italian version of *Jeopardy!*, was a huge success with 20 to 30 million viewers every Thursday night, the highest audience in the history of Italian television.

The hits followed over the next three decades resulting in 24 Telegatto awards.

On his 80th birthday in 2004 he was appointed Great Official at the Merit of Italian Republic by the then Italian President Carlo Azeglio Ciampi.

He begins all his shows with his trademark greeting: "Allegria!" ("Cheers!").

———◆———

ANTHROPOLOGICAL MICHAELS

Michael Harkin specialises in the Heiltsuk people centred on the island communities of Bella Bella and Klemtu of British Columbia, Canada.

Descended from a number of tribal groups who came together in the 19th century and came to be called the Bella Bella Indians, the Heiltsuk culture is known for its ceremonial, military and artistic skills. They also got a bit of a reputation as hustlers, demanding extra large blankets from visiting traders, cutting them to standards size for re-trade and sewing the extra pieces together to make more blankets.

In the 1970s, American **Michael Harner** suggested the Aztecs had resorted to organised cannibalism on a vast scale to make up for an assumed protein deficiency in the diet.

Michael Taussig's seminal work, *Shamanism, Colonialism and the Wild Man: A Study in Terror and Healing*, examines Colonialism in South America. Famous for his dramatic lectures, the anthropologist once gave a talk with his head in a paper bag (a homage to a Dadaist artist).

<hr />

ARCHITECT MICHAELS

The Paragon in Blackheath, London, was designed by famous Regency architect **Michael Searles** (1750-1813). The 14-house crescent – Grade 1 listed buildings – comprises seven blocks of semi-detached houses, each linked by a single story colonnade, with a lodge house at each end.

Sir Michael Hopkins, the English architect, designed the new opera house at Glyndebourne, the Mound Stand at Lord's Cricket Ground and the extension to the Manchester City Art Gallery.

Michael J. Fox played architect Frank Bannister in the 1996 film, *Frighteners*, a comedy/horror film about a psychic private detective. After a car accident in which his wife, Debra, was killed and he was injured, Bannister develops psychic abilities allowing him to see, hear, and communicate with ghosts.

In the American television series *The Brady Bunch*, **Mike Brady** is head of the fictional family. The widowed architect became the stepfather of Carol Brady's three daughters when he married Carol Martin. He was once approached to design a powder-puff shaped factory.

Adam Sandler played an architect in the 2006 film, *Click*. The workaholic **Michael** finds a universal remote that allows him to fast-forward and rewind to different parts of his life. Complications arise when the remote starts to overrule his choices. The film was nominated for an Academy Award for Best Make-up.

The Jonathan Reeves character in *White Noise* (2005) was played by **Michael Keaton**. The pregnant wife of the architect disappears after a car accident near a cliff. Weeks later, a mysterious man says his wife is dead and has communicated with him through Electronic Voice Phenomena.

Johann Michael Fischer (1692-1766) was a German architect in the late Baroque period and designed 32 churches and 23 monasteries in southern Germany.

Famous for his controversial 'Earthships', **Michael Reynolds** is a pioneering American architect. Specialising in sustainable living, he has spent over thirty years constructing buildings from aluminium cans, plastic and glass bottles, and old car tyres. The method involves no recycling, as such, as the items are used as they are found by turning them into 'bricks' and filling cavities with earth.

Since the early 1970s, Reynolds has fought legislation from New Mexico state authorities and had his architect's licence revoked in 2000. After, reluctantly, complying with rigid rules, he can now practice again.

The onslaught of global warming has made the designs – which regulate temperature, wherever they are built, and require no mains electricity, water or sanitation pipes – very popular throughout the world.

ASTRONAUT MICHAELS

Michael Adams: (1930-1967)
The astronaut reached an altitude of 266,000 feet
(50.38 miles) on his solo X-15-3 flight on November 15.
Ten minutes and 35 seconds after launch, the aircraft
broke up northeast of the town of Johannesburg and
wreckage was discovered near Cuddeback Lake in
California.

Michael Baker (b. 1953), now retired, has spent a total 40
days, 4 hours and 59 minutes in space.

Michael 'Bloomer' Bloomfield (b. 1959) resigned from
NASA in July 2007 after 32 days, 11 hours, and 2 minutes
in space.

Michael 'Rich' Clifford (b. 1952), once orbited the
Earth 145 times on the Atlantis spacecraft in 1996. The
American astronaut completed 27 days, 18 hours and 24
minutes in space.

Major General Michael Collins (b. 1930) was the
first Italian/American in space, was part of the Apollo 11
mission, and has spent a total of 11 days, 2 hours and 4
minutes in space.

In 1968, Collins noticed a problem with his legs. His knee would almost give way walking down stairs and felt strange in hot and cold water. The diagnosis was a cervical disc herniation that was cured by fusing two vertebrae together.

Michael Foale (b. 1957) is a NASA astronaut who holds the record for most time spent in space by a UK and US citizen: 374 days, 11 hours and 19 minutes. He is a veteran of six space shuttle missions and extended stays on both Mir and the International Space Station and was the first Briton to perform a space walk.

Michael Edward Fossum (b. 1957) is an American astronaut who entered space for the first time on July 4th, 2006. A junior high school in McAllen, Texas has been named after him.

Michael Landon Gernhardt (b. 1956) has logged over 43 days in space and also has over 700 deep sea dives to his name.

Miguel 'LA' López-Alegría (b. 1958) is an American/ Spanish astronaut. He has been in space over 257 days in total, including a 251-day 'Expedition 14' mission aboard the International Space Station.

Michael James Massimino (b. 1962) broke a space-walking record with 35 hours and 55 minutes during five spacewalks on STS-109 Columbia – the fourth Hubble Space Telescope (HST) servicing mission – in 2002.

Michael James McCulley is a retired NASA astronaut who clocked up 4 days, 23 hours and 39 minutes away from planet Earth. He lists his hobbies as skiing, reading, camping, and jogging.

NOTABLE MICHAELS

Michael Brown
Astronomer Michael Brown and his team have discovered many trans-Neptunian objects (TNOs) including Eris, the first TNO discovered that is larger than Pluto.

Michael DeWayne Brown
Michael DeWayne Brown was Undersecretary of Emergency Preparedness and Response (EP&R) and was appointed in January, 2003 by President George W. Bush. He resigned in September, 2005 following public outcry over his handling of Hurricane Katrina.

Michael Leunig
Michael Leunig is a celebrated Australian cartoonist and is best known for works including The Adventures of Vasco Pajama and the Curly Flats series. He was declared one of Australia's Living Treasures by the National Trust of Australia in 1999 and has also had a Melbourne tram named after him.

Michael Florentius van Langren

Michael Florentius van Langren (1600-1675) was a Dutch astronomer and cartographer. He attempted to determine longitude by observing the position of the Moon which led him to produce the first ever map of Earth's only natural satellite. Langrenus crater on the Moon was named for him.

Michael Bach

Michael Bach (1808-1878) was a German entomologist specialising in Coleoptera (the study of beetles).

Michael Okuda

The animated computer displays for the Enterprise-A bridge in *Star Trek IV: The Voyage Home*, were designed by the graphic designer Michael Okuda who also served as a technical consultant on the series.

Mick Mannock

Major Edward Corringham 'Mick' Mannock was a British First World War flying ace and posthumous recipient of the Victoria Cross. Mick was possibly the highest-scoring British Empire ace of the war, ahead of Billy Bishop (72 kills). Regarded as one of the greatest fighter pilots of the war, Mannock's name features on the front of a Brighton & Hove bus.

MINTED MICHAELS

Over 100 Michaels featured in the *Sunday Times* Rich List of 2008. At the top is **Michael Spencer** with a £1,150m fortune, and in equal 1,794th position are Michelle and Michael Mone who have a significant stake in MJM – inventors of the Ultimo bra – worth £40million.

The only Michael in the 'Young' list was **Andrew Michael**, founder of Fasthosts, one of Britain's largest web-hosting companies. He started the company in his bedroom as a 17-year-old in 1997 and sold it to the German service provider United Internet for approximately £61m ten years later.

Michael Rubens Bloomberg (b. 1942) is an American businessman, philanthropist, and the Mayor of New York City, a role he is remunerated for at one dollar per year.

His net worth is US$11.5 billion as of 2007 and he was ranked 34th by Forbes magazine in its list of 400 Richest Americans in 2006.

As of 2008, 56-year-old **Michael Lee-Chin** was worth $1.6bn with a personal property portfolio including 250 acres of beachfront property in Ocho Rios, Jamaica and homes in Canada and Florida.

Born in Chemno in the Nazi occupied Poland of 1943,
Michael Otto is the head of Otto Group, the world's largest
mail order company. Thanks to ever-increasing Internet sales,
the company maintains its position as the World Wide Web's
second-biggest retailer, behind Amazon.com.

Michael Herz is head of the family-owned Tchibo
Holding, one of Germany's largest retail groups, including
Tchibo, a chain of coffee shops/cafés.

Michael Dell (b. 1965) founded Dell Inc. – as PCs Limited
– in 1984. He had his first encounter with a computer at
the age of 15 when he broke down a brand new Apple II
machine and rebuilt it, just to see if he could. The company
employ over 78,000 staff across the globe.

Ranked 62nd on the *Sunday Times* Rich List 2008 with
a wealth of £1.5 billion, **Michael Spencer** runs Icap
(Intercapital), the world's biggest inter-dealer broker.
While still a student at Corpus Christi College, Oxford,
he made £300 in shares and switched his attentions from
science to finance.

Born in St Helens in 1936, **Sir Michael Smurfit** joined
his father's company Jefferson Smurfit & Sons Ltd in 1955.
He created Ireland's first international company which grew
to become a global leader in paper-based packaging.

Despite not holding an academic degree – apart from an honorary Doctor of Laws – the businessman is often referred to as Dr. Michael Smurfit. Recipients of honorary degrees are not generally entitled to use the title 'Doctor' resulting in much controversy and amusement in Ireland.

In 2008, **Michael Flatley** celebrated his fiftieth year. The American dancer who specialises in the traditional steps of his parents' birthplace – Ireland – moved to Chicago as a child. Both his mother and grandmother were champion Irish dancers. Initially reluctant to follow in their footsteps, the young Flatley discovered a natural ability and in 1975 became the first non-European resident to win the All-Ireland Championship for Irish dance. As a trained boxer, he won the Chicago Golden Gloves Championship in the same year!

As the intermission act during the 1994 Eurovision Song Contest, Flatley performed a shortened version of what was to become the hugely popular *Riverdance* with Jean Butler. Successful productions followed including *Lord of the Dance*, *Feet of Flames* and *Celtic Tiger*.

Flatley, who is worth £350 million, always keeps an empty chair for his grandmother in the front row of all his concerts, as a sign of remembrance.

DISAPPEARING MICHAELS

On November 17th, 1961, **Michael Rockefeller** – a member of the famous family – and Dutch anthropologist René Wassing were in a dugout canoe about three miles from shore in the Asmat region of south-western New Guinea when their vessel was swamped and overturned. After drifting for some time, Rockefeller said to his companion, "I think I can make it" and swam for dry land. He was never seen again and was finally declared dead in 1964.

⇒◆⇐

"You can't succeed unless you've got failure, especially creatively."
Michael Dammann Eisner, *former CEO, The Walt Disney Company.*

⇒◆⇐

CHECKMATE MICHAELS

Michael John Basman (b. 1946) is an English chess player – his father was an Armenian immigrant – who was crowned International Master in 1980. He created the UK Chess Challenge, a tournament for juniors of all standards and ages progressing over 4 stages. His family knew the singer Cleo Laine, who babysat the young Michael.

Michael Roy Freeman moved to New Zealand as a 19-year-old in 1979. He gained his Senior International Master title in 2003.

Michael Rohde (b. 1959) achieved his master rating at the age of 13 and he eventually got his grandmaster title in 1988.

Michael Roiz (born 1983 in Russia) learned to play chess at seven years old and finished second in the national championship under-10 category, aged nine and became a grandmaster in 2003.

<hr/>

PROMINENT MICHAELS IN GAELIC FOOTBALL

Mick O'Dwyer is one of the most decorated managers and former players in Irish Gaelic football history winning 12 Munster, and 4 All-Ireland titles.

As manager, **Mickey Harte** has led Tyrone to two All-Ireland titles and is considered by many to be one of the most shrewd and cunning tacticians in the game.

Regarded as one of the greatest Gaelic footballers players of all-time, **Mick O'Connell** was born on Valentia Island – one of Europe's westernmost inhabited locations, approximately 11km long by 3km wide and the site of the first permanent communications link, a cross-ocean cable, between Europe and America in 1857 – and played for Kerry from 1956 until 1973.

———◈———

WHAT DOES MICHAEL MEAN, EXACTLY?

(www.urbandictionary.com)

A lonely, desperate male who seeks out and dates older women on the internet.

USAGE:
*"**Michael** was a little socially awkward so he decided to pursue online relationships instead of real ones and finally found his partner and mother figure in a popular internet chat room."*

———◈———

SLAMDUNK THE MICHAEL

Michael Adams	5ft 10ins.
Michael Anderson	5ft 11ins.
Michael Bradley	6ft 10ins.
Michael Cage	6ft 9ins.
Michael Cooper	6ft 7ins.
Michael Curry	6ft 5ins.
Michael Dickerson	6ft 5ins.
Michael Doleac	6ft 11ins.
Michael Finley	6ft 7ins.
Michael Hawkins	6ft 0ins.
Michael Jackson	6ft 2ins.

Michael Olowokandi	7ft 0ins.
Michael 'Silky' Redd	6ft 6ins.
Michael Ruffin	6ft 8ins.
Michael Smith	6ft 10ins.
Michael 'Yogi' Stewart	6ft 10ins.
Michael Sweetney	6ft 8ins.
Michael Wiley	6ft 9ins.

PUTTING MICHAELS

A leading administrator in world golf in the late 20th
century, **Sir Michael Bonallack** (b. 1934) was an English
amateur golfer. He was inducted into the World Golf
Hall of Fame in 2000 and once finished 11th in the Open
Championship.

Michael Shane Campbell is a Maori golfer from New
Zealand who in 2005 won both the US Open and the £1
million World Matchplay championship. He is a great-
great-great-grandson of John Logan Campbell, a Scottish
emigrant who became mayor of Auckland in 1901.

Michael Christie died of a self-inflicted wound, aged 34,
on April 22nd, 2004. Nine years earlier the American golfer
shot a tournament record 22 under par to win the Carolina
Classic, his first professional victory.

After playing over 250 events on the PGA Tour, with two second place, and three third place finishes, **Michael Allen** is yet to register a victory (as at March 2009).

Michael Clark II was PGA Tour Rookie of the Year in 2000 but five years later was back on the Nationwide Tour, aged 36.

Northern Irishman **Michael Hoey** had a disappointing rookie season on the European Tour in 2006, losing his card. He regained confidence with the second Challenge Tour victory of his career at the 2007 Tessali-Metaponto Open di Puglia e Basilicata in Italy.

In June 2003, Swede **Michael Jonzon** won his first Challenge Tour title in the Galeria Kaufhof Pokal Challenge in Germany.

Ankylosing spondylitis – known as bamboo spine, a degenerative inflammatory arthritis – affects the back and curtailed the golf career of Englishman **Michael King** who won a solitary European Tour title at the SOS Talisman TPC in 1979.

Frenchman **Michael Lorenzo-Vera** is equally at home on the golf course or on the beaches of his native Biarritz. The 6ft 10ins. golfer set a Challenge Tour record in 2007 earning €128,927.

The Hon. Michael Scott OBE (1878-1959) was an English amateur golfer, most famous for being the oldest winner of The Amateur Championship, at the age of 55, in 1933.

<hr>

ILLUSTRATING MICHAELS

Michael Hague (born 1948) has illustrated *The Wind in the Willows*, *The Wizard of Oz* and the stories of Hans Christian Andersen.

Michael Mathias Prechtl (died, aged 76, in 2003) was a German artist, illustrator and cartoonist who served as a soldier on the Eastern Front during World War II and spent 1945-49 as a prisoner of war in the Soviet Union. He is famous for illustrating German editions of literary classics such as works by E.T.A. Hoffmann, Thomas More, Dante, Goethe, Benvenuto Cellini, and the letters of Mozart and achieved notoriety for his front-page work on *Der Spiegel* – meaning 'The Mirror', Europe's biggest and most influential weekly magazine, published in Hamburg, with a circulation of more than one million per week – in the 1980s.

Multiple-award-winning American artist **Michael Whelan** has worked on over 350 book and magazine covers, including most of the Del Rey editions of Anne McCaffrey's *Dragonriders of Pern* series and Edgar Rice

Burroughs' *Barsoom* series, plus interior illustrations for Stephen King's *The Gunslinger(The Dark Tower)*, the first and last of the *Dark Tower* books.

He also illustrated the cover for Meat Loaf's 1993 album Bat out of Hell II: Back into Hell.

Michael 'Lippy' Lipman is the storyboard artist, animator and director of Happy Tree Friends. The flash cartoon series has gained a cult following after becoming an internet phenomenon. "Not recommended for small children or big babies", the show features cute characters whose everyday activities always end up in violent and gruesome deaths.

WHAT DOES MICHAEL MEAN, EXACTLY?
(www.urbandictionary.com)

An online term used to describe a homosexual new to the gay community. Could also be applied to males who appear more feminine in personality, or appearance.
Can also be applied to transgenders.

USAGE:
*"We welcomed **Michael** into our community."*

HARD AS NAILS MICHAELS

Renowned for his dyed blond hair, gladiator trunks and lithe physique, **Michael 'The Black Sniper' McDonald** (b. 1965) is a Canadian kickboxer.

In 1996, he won his first professional fight in Regina, Saskatchewan, knocking out his local opponent in just 30 seconds.

Mick Foley, Sr. is widely regarded as the greatest professional wrestler in World Wrestling Federation history. Born in 1965, Foley played truant from school to see his idol, Jimmy 'Superfly' Snuka in New York City. Wrestling from his 21st birthday, Foley has won everything in the game and enjoys the occasional bout, but now concentrates on his autobiographical and fiction writing.

On March 16th, 1994, Foley was stuck in the ring ropes during a fight and as he struggled to release himself, he tore off two-thirds of his ear. Later that year he had to choose between reattaching his ear or wrestling in a title contest. Foley chose to wrestle, and won.

CHILDREN'S TV MICHAELS

English actor **Michael Angelis** (b. 1952) narrated the British *Thomas the Tank Engine & Friends* from 1991 to 2007, and six American Thomas episodes in 2003 before being replaced by **Michael Brandon**. He was once married to *Coronation Street* actress Helen Worth, who plays Gail Platt.

The Metal Mickey TV Show ran from 1980 to 1983. The show centred around a five feet tall fictional robot – which made its first television appearance in the ITV children's magazine show *The Saturday Banana* in 1978 – created by a child, who was a science boffin, to help out around the house.

Some episodes of the show were produced and directed by **Micky Dolenz**, formerly of The Monkees.

Mike and Angelo ran on Children's ITV between 1989 and 2000. Angelo the alien came from another world, the portal of which was a wardrobe in a bedroom. He lived with a young boy called **Mike** (played by **Michael Benz**). The show ran for 123 episodes and concentrated on the havoc wreaked by the two who would summon up historical figures from the past.

Michael Cole wrote and produced *Heads and Tails* for the BBC in the late 1970s. The music and voices were famously provided by Derek Griffiths. Cole also penned *Over the Moon Pie, Playboard, Pie in the Sky* and *Ragtime* and worked on *Fingerbobs*.

Michael Bond's animated creation, *The Herbs*, was first aired in 1968. Characters included Parsley the Lion, Dill the Dog, Sage the Owl, Bayleaf the Gardener, Constable Knapweed, Mr and Mrs Onion and The Chives, Aunt Mint, Tarragon the Dragon, Belladonna, the evil witch and deadly nightshade flower.

The magic word "Herbidacious" would start another adventure of animals living in the walled English country garden of Sir Basil and Lady Rosemary.

Parsley the Lion went on to have his own spin-off series called *The Adventures of Parsley*, which began in 1970. Thirty-two five-minute episodes were made.

Stop – Go! involved a whole team of **Michaels**.
The 13 programmes, made from Christmas Eve 1984, were edited by **Michael Williamson**, produced by **Michael Cole**, while the music was arranged by **Michael Omer**, who also worked on *Scragtag & His Tea-Time Telly*.

Charlie Chalk, a circus clown, is shipwrecked on an island and makes friends with its strange inhabitants. **Michael Williams** – who appeared alongside wife Judi Dench in the situation comedy, *A Fine Romance*, from 1981 onwards – provided the voices of the woodland animals. He was awarded a Knighthood of St. Gregory by Pope John Paul II shortly before his death from lung cancer at the age of 65 in 2001.

⇒◆⇐

WHAT DOES MIKE MEAN, EXACTLY?
(www.urbandictionary.com)

A gay prostitute who looks like a gorilla and is usually found selling his wares for a few pence around colleges.

USAGE:
Child One: "What's that kid doing there?"
Child Two: "Leave him alone, he's a male prostitute, a Mike."

⇒◆⇐

GLOBAL FOOTBALLING MICHAELS

As at early 2008, the following Michaels were plying their trade at:

Sivasspor: Turkish Super Premier League
Michael Petkovic (b. 1976)

An Australian goalkeeper of Serbian descent. His brother, Jason, played in goal for Perth Glory.

Apoel FC: Cyprus Football League
Chrysis Michael (b. 1977)

A Cypriot international midfielder.

LASK Linz: Austrian league First Division
Michael Baur (b. 1969)

Played nearly 400 games – interspersed with a seven-game spell at Urawa Red Diamonds (Japan) – for Tirol Innsbruck.

FC Copenhagen: Danish Superliga
Dane **Michael Gravgaard** (b. 1978)

Normally plays at centre-back, but can also operate as a striker. On June 2, 2007, he stopped the attacking Denmark fan in the 2008 UEFA qualifier international match against Sweden which was subsequently abandoned.

Aalborg Boldspilklub: Danish Superliga
Danish defender **Michael Jakobsen** (b. 1986)

Awarded the Danish Under-17 Player of the Year award in 2002.

Rosenborg: Norwegian Premier League
Michael Jamtfall (b. 1987)

A striker and the son of Jørn Jamtfall, a former goalkeeper turned coach.

De Graafschap: Eredivisie, Holland
Nijmegen-born **Michael Jansen** (b. 1984)

A Dutch defender. He lost consciousness after suffering cardiac arrhythmia – abnormal electrical activity in the heart – on May 15, 2005 in a match versus Ajax.

Coventry City: Championship, England
Maltese striker **Michael Mifsud** (b. 1981)

Previously played for Sliema Wanderers, Kaiserslautern and Lillestrøm and was voted Maltese Sports Person of the Year in 2001 and 2003.

Karlsruher SC: German Bundesliga
German midfielder **Michael Mutzel** (b. 1979)

Played for FC Augsburg, Eintracht Frankfurt and VfB Stuttgart since 1997.

Melbourne Victory: Hyundai A-League, Australia
Goalkeeper **Michael Theoklitos** (b. 1981)

Of Greek ancestry, has enjoyed three different spells at Whittlesea Zebras, a merger of the Box Hill Inter, Brunswick Juventus (former National League Champions) and Bulleen Lions clubs.

SpVgg Weiden: Oberliga Bayern, Germany
German midfielder **Michael Wiesinger** (b. 1972)
Won the Bundesliga twice – 2000, and 2001 – with Bayern
Munich.

Beitar Jerusalem: Ligat ha'Al, Israeli Premier League
Michael Zandberg (Sandberg means 'sand mountain' in
German/Yiddish) was born in 1980.

The Israeli winger was set to sign a $600,000 one-year
contract with Sheffield United, but decided against the move
when the Blades were relegated from the Premiership in 2007.

ONE CLUB MICHAELS

Michael Buskermolen (b. 1972) spent his entire 16-year
career at AZ Alkmaar of Holland. The Dutchman, also
known as 'Mr AZ', played 399 league games for the club.

Michael Zorc (b. 1962) played 463 games (a club record),
between 1981 and 1998, for Borussia Dortmund. The
German was nicknamed 'Susi', because of his long hair at
the start of his career, and was an excellent penalty-taker.

Mike Davies (b. 1966) enjoyed a football career beside
the seaside. The flame-haired Englishman occupied many
positions during his 310 games for Blackpool.

WHAT DOES MICK MEAN, EXACTLY?

(www.urbandictionary.com)

A freestyle biking term used to describe an exceptionally
slow wheelie manoeuvre, in particular, without the
protection of a helmet.

USAGE:
*"My friends and I posted up some pictures of us doing **Micks** and
Endos in a car park yesterday. People gave us a hard time because
someone wasn't wearing a helmet in one of the pictures."*

ODD SHAPED BALL MICHAELS

Born in County Kerry, Ireland, in 1941, **Mick Doyle**
played rugby for his country and had the distinction of
never being dropped during his 20-cap career as a flanker.

He studied veterinary science at University College Dublin, and
made his international debut against France on January 23rd
1965, scoring a try. Under Doyle's stewardship, Ireland won the
Triple Crown and Five Nations Championship in 1985.

Doyle was killed in a car crash in Dungannon on May 11th
2004, aged 62.

Named as one of the world's greatest players of all time
by *The Times* – and also the third-greatest All Black of all
time after Colin Meads and Sean Fitzpatrick – **Michael**

Niko Jones was born in Auckland, New Zealand in 1965.

Jones' career was blighted by injuries and his international career was also affected by his strong Christian beliefs. He refused to play on Sundays. As a result, he missed three games during the 1987 and 1991 Rugby World Cups.

Born in Vancouver, Canada in 1973, **Mike James** has represented his country, in the lock (second row) position, in four Rugby World Cups: 1995, 1999, 2003 and 2007.

———⟨◆⟩———

WHAT DOES MICK MEAN, EXACTLY?
(www.urbandictionary.com)

Underground Melbourne slang: verb; to vomit in the urinal at a bar, especially when the sheer volume of vomit blocks the drain.

USAGE:
1. *"Blimey, mate, I just chucked the worst Mick ever."*
2. *"Look out! He's going to Mick!"*

———⟨◆⟩———

MICHAEL DRINKS

The Mickey Slim...
...enjoyed a short-lived popularity in the United States in the 1940s and 1950s.

It was made by combining gin with a pinch of DDT (also known as dichlorodiphenyltrichloroethane), an insecticide that would later be banned in most countries; consumers of this concoction claimed that its effects were similar to absinthe.

Mickey Finn...

...is essentially a sedative drug slipped surreptitiously into someone's drink. The phrase originated, supposedly, after a character from Chicago. Finn was the keeper of the city's Lone Star Saloon in the late 19th and early 20th century and he was alleged to have drugged and robbed his customers.

Chicago Daily News: *"The complete defence advanced by* **Mickey Finn**, *proprietor of the Lone Star saloon ... described ... as the scene of blood-curdling crimes through the agency of drugged liquor."*

⬅◆➡

"Earlier on today, apparently, a woman rang the BBC and said she heard there was a hurricane on the way... well, if you're watching, don't worry, there isn't!"
Michael Fish, *a few hours before the storm broke, on Thursday 15th October 1987*

ALL AT SEA MICHAELS

Michiel Adriaenszoon de Ruyter (1607-1676) was a famous Dutch admiral.

He is best known for leading his countrymen in a successful raid on English naval ships during the Second Anglo-Dutch War at the Battle of Medway, in June 1667.

They burnt three capital ships and ten lesser naval vessels and towed away the *Unity* and the *Royal Charles*, pride and normal flagship of the English fleet.

≡≡◆≡≡

PAINTING MICHAELS

Michael Coxcie (1499-1592) was a Flemish painter who painted the chapel of Cardinal Enckenvoirt in the church of Santa Maria dell' Anima. He was known as the Flemish Raphael and died, in his home-town of Mechelen, after falling from a flight of stairs.

Creator of the painting technique known as Rectoversion (1991) – based on a French neologism which literally means "rotation of the front side (recto)" – **Michel De Caso** (b. 1956) is a visual artist born in Toulouse, France.

Michael Feuchtmayer (b. 1667) was a member of the Feuchtmayer family of Baroque artists and was the brother of Franz Joseph and Johann Michael Feuchtmayer (the Elder).

German artist **Michael Sowa** (b. 1945) is renowned for his whimsical paintings including 'Laptop Sheep', 'Schone Allee Im Norden Von Berlin', 'Mann, Fisch, Tisch' and 'Homo Sapiens'.

Irish-American painter **William Michael Harnett** was born during the 1848 potato famine in Ireland. He is famed for his style: trompe l'oeil (literally, "fool the eye").

Still-lifes of ordinary objects, arranged on a ledge or hanging from a nail, are painted in such a way that the painting can be mistaken for the objects themselves.

Born in Mexico City, **José Miguel Covarrubias** (1904-1957) was a Mexican painter and caricaturist, ethnologist and art historian who moved to New York City aged 20. He drew for several top magazines, married the dancer Rosa Roland, and then took a trip to south-east Asia (Java, Bali, India and Vietnam), Africa and Europe as a Guggenheim Fellow.

Swedish painter, **Michael Dahl** was born in Stockholm on Thursday 29th September 1659. He moved to London, aged 23, for a three-year stay and, from 1685, travelled and worked in Paris, Venice, Rome and Frankfurt.

Dahl's most important works are housed at the National Maritime Museum, London; a series of portraits of contemporary admirals. Having converted to Roman Catholicism during his time in Rome, he was suspected of being a Jacobite sympathiser and lost all favour at the court under the Hanoverians. He died in London in 1743, two years after his son Michael, who had also been a painter.

Michael Goldberg, an abstract painter of the New York School whose vibrant works are in major museums and private collections, died in Manhattan in 2007, aged 83. In his youth, he was never expected to make money at his painting and created art just for himself. Buyers began to appear in the mid 1950s when the collector Walter P. Chrysler Jr. bought $10,000 worth of his work. Unemployed at the time, with no bank account, Michael received the first payment on a freezing winter day. His first act was to buy an electric blanket and then spent the rest of the weekend in bed, the money tucked beneath his arm.

⋙◆⋘

WHAT DOES MIKE MEAN, EXACTLY?
(www.urbandictionary.com)

The best boyfriend in the world.

Mike is one bad son of a gun. He goes skinny dipping and laughs himself to sleep.

USAGE:
"Wow! You are sooo Mike!"

STREAKING MICHAELS

In April 1974 Australian **Michael O'Brien** became the first recorded streaker at Twickenham. The bearded 25-year-old's assets were famously covered by a policeman's helmet during the Five Nations rugby match between England and France.

Michael Angelow, wearing only plimsolls, took his life into his own hands at Lord's Cricket Ground in August 1975 when he hurdled the stumps as England faced Australia in the fourth day of the second Test.

The veteran radio commentator John Arlott, who had not been fully briefed on the new British craze, proclaimed: "It's a freaker".

Angelow was fined £10.

⇒◆⇐

FAMOUS ANIMALS CALLED MICHAEL

Michael was a 'talking' gorilla who learnt over 600 gestures in American Sign Language, taught to him by Koko, a female gorilla – initially intended to be his mate, but she wasn't interested – and other staff at Stanford University.

The 205kg animal, an orphan, spent most of his life at The Gorilla Foundation, just south of San Francisco. He died aged 27, on April 19th 2000.

"We are deeply saddened by the loss of our dear friend Michael. He has been an inspiration to us all. He had a great facility with gestural communication and was a talented artist," said Francine Patterson, the foundation's president.

⬤

TINKLING MICHAELS

Michael Endres (b. 1961) – who specialises in Mozart, Schubert, Schumann and Ravel – is considered one of Germany's top pianists. He has recorded the 400 dances of Franz Schubert and has received many prizes including Choc du Musique and Diapason.

Michael Raucheisen, who died in 1984 aged 95, was a German pianist. His musical development was so important to the family – he was an only child – they moved to Munich. A musical innovator, he played his accompaniments with the piano lid open in order to obtain a better tonal balance between the voice and the instrument.

Michael Cain attended the University of North Texas (UNT) before composing for, and performing with, artists such as Marlena Shaw, Bobby McFerrin, and Don Alias.

A pioneering English jazz pianist and composer, **Michael Garrick** (b. 1933) was an entirely self-taught musician. He is best known for his jazz-choral works, the first of which he started in 1967, Jazz Praises, and for his interest in Indian classical music.

Michael 'Dodo' Marmarosa began his bebop pianist career, aged just 15, with the Johnny "Scat" Davis Orchestra in 1941. Classically trained, he received his uncomplimentary nickname as a child because of his large head and short body.

After 1950, his only recording was a 1961 session for Argo Records under the supervision of Chicago producer Jack Tracy (*Dodo's Back!*). His low profile was attributed to mental illness; Marmarosa was drafted in 1954, given electric shock treatment, and discharged in poor psychological condition.

Celluloid Michaels

Youngest of the three Penn brothers – Chris died in 2006 while eldest sibling Sean continues to act – **Michael** is a singer/songwriter who once appeared as an extra in hospital drama *St. Elsewhere*.

His music was once described by *Vox* magazine critic Gary Leboff as: "pig-headedly uncommercial".

Played by comedic actor Paul Hogan, **Michael J. 'Crocodile' Dundee** is a fictional character from the Australian outback who has never been to a city in his life. Supposedly born in a cave, in the Northern Territory, and raised by Aborigines, he meets an American reporter who takes him back to the States. Much mirth and hilarity ensue as Mick ingratiates himself with the locals by throwing a can of baked beans at a thief etc.

Born in Edmonton, Canada in 1961, pint-sized actor **Michael J. Fox** – who added his middle initial in homage of Michael J. Pollard – made his professional Canadian TV debut in the sitcom *Leo and Me* in 1976.

He shot to fame in *Family Ties* where he won three Emmy Awards and a Golden Globe playing money-obsessed Alex P. Keaton. He married co-star Tracey Pollan is 1988 and the couple have four children.

Fox, as Marty McFly, is perhaps best known for his starring role in the three *Back to the Future* films. He was diagnosed with Parkinson's disease in 1991 after noticing symptoms on the set of *Doc Hollywood*. Fox stopped acting in 2006 after providing the voice of Stuart Little in the eponymous film, and a successful run in *Spin City*.

American actor **Michael Douglas** – born on September 25th, 1944, exactly 25 years after his Welsh wife Catherine Zeta-Jones – first hit our TV screens as a young policeman alongside Karl Malden in *The Streets of San Francisco*.

As well as being a successful actor with a string of Hollywood blockbusters under his belt, the reformed sex addict is also an accomplished producer with credits including the Oscar winning *One Flew Over the Cuckoo's Nest* and *Romancing The Stone*.

In 1997 Douglas' caddy, James Parker, sued him for $155 million after the New Yorker accused the *Fatal Attraction* star of hitting him in the groin with an errant golf ball, rupturing Parker's testicle. The case was later settled out of court.

American actor, writer, director, and producer, **Michael Landon** starred in three popular TV series; *Bonanza* (1959-1973), *Little House on the Prairie* (1974-1983), and *Highway to Heaven* (1984-1989).

During his childhood, Michael witnessed his mother attempt suicide by jumping off a cliff. She displayed his wet sheets – he suffered from bed-wetting – for all to see and the youngster would run home every day to remove them before his classmates saw.

Renowned for his sense of humour, Michael fathered nine children and once dressed as a superhero to visit a pizza parlour.

Michael Imperioli (b. 1966) is best known for his role as Christopher Moltisanti on *The Sopranos*. He was Tony Soprano's protégé and a Capo (caporegime) – a term used in the Mafia for a high ranking made member of a crime family who heads a 'crew' of soldiers and has major social status and influence in the organisation – and was killed by his 'uncle' at the end of series 6.

The two were injured in a severe car accident while driving back from a meeting with the New York crew. Christopher lost control of his vehicle and rolled several times before coming to a stop in a ditch. He was not wearing a seat belt and suffered internal injuries.

Instead of calling for help, and after noticing that a branch had impaled the baby seat in the back where Christopher's daughter could have been sitting – plus the fact he was bleeding through his mouth – Tony pinched his nostrils and suffocated him.

The Emmy-winning and Golden Globe Award-nominated Imperioli spent the 2008-2009 television season as Officer Ray Carling in the US version of *Life on Mars*.

Born in 1946, **Michael Tucci** is perhaps most famous for his role as the T-Birds' Sonny in the smash hit film *Grease*.

He played Pete Schumaker on *It's Garry Shandling's Show* for five years to 1990, spent more than three years touring with musical *Chicago*, and also featured as hospital administrator Norman Briggs, Dick Van Dyke's friend, on daytime American TV show *Diagnosis: Murder*.

Synonymous with 1980s geek, **Michael Hall** (b. 1968) has happily diversified after appearing as the brainy Brian Johnson in 1985's *The Breakfast Club*, where he met, and subsequently dated, co-star Molly Ringwald.

He was, and remains, the youngest cast member in the history of *Saturday Night Live* after joining the cast as a 17-year-old.

He was cast as a villain in 1990's *Edward Scissorhands* and played Gotham City television reporter **Mike Engel** in *The Dark Knight*.

MICHAELS BORN IN **1800**

Michael Gottlieb Birckner Bindesbøll – Danish architect
Etienne-Michel Faillon – French Catholic historian
Michail Spyromilios – Greek soldier and politician
Mikhail Petrovich Pogodin – Russian historian and journalist

BEHIND THE CAMERA MICHAELS

After beginning work at Granada television as a 23-year-old trainee in 1964, **Michael Apted**'s first assignment was for the famous *Up* series which followed fourteen 7-year-old children from different socio-economic backgrounds. The programme has followed their lives with an update show every seven years thereafter. The next instalment, *56 Up*, is due to be shown in 2009/10.

Despite being an Academy Award-winning film director, **Michael Cimino**'s career was characterised by spectacular successes, and abject failures.

Born in New York City in 1939, the Yale University graduate was behind the camera for the Oscar-winning *The Deer Hunter* (1978) for which he received two Academy Awards – Best Director and Best Picture. His next film was the disastrous *Heaven's Gate* (1980) which came in several times over budget, nearly bankrupting the studio.

He was in charge on the set of *Footloose* for four months but was replaced by Herbert Ross after making extravagant demands on the overall production, and to the set constructors.

The prolific and energetic Hungarian-American film director **Michael Curtiz** directed at least fifty films in Europe and a further hundred in the United States, before passing away in 1961. He is best known for his work on *The*

Adventures of Robin Hood, *Angels with Dirty Faces*, *Casablanca*, *Yankee Doodle Dandy* and *White Christmas*.

He was born Manó Kertész Kaminer to a Jewish family in Budapest, Hungary – supposedly in 1886 – and would brag of representing the country of his birth in fencing at the 1912 Olympic Games.

Curtiz worked hard and often criticised actors for taking lunch. Bette Davis refused to work with him again after he called her a "goddamned nothing no good sexless son of a bitch".

Best known for his bleak and disturbing style, German-born **Michael Haneke** is an Austrian filmmaker and writer whose breakthrough came with his 1992 feature film *Benny's Video*: a young man, virtually ignored by his wealthy parents, spends his time in his bedroom obsessively watching violent films (including his home video of a pig being slaughtered). He slips into further madness killing a girl with a stun gun and filming it.

American **Michael Lehmann** has directed *The Outsiders* (1983), *Heathers* (1989), *Hudson Hawk* (1991), *Airheads* (1994), *The Truth About Cats & Dogs* (1996), and *Because I Said So* (2007). His TV credits include *The West Wing* and *The Larry Sanders Show*.

Famous for making three of the five highest-grossing documentaries of all time, **Michael Moore** was born in Flint, Michigan in 1954. He dropped out of university and founded the alternative weekly magazine *The Flint Voice*, which soon changed its name to *The Michigan Voice* as it expanded to cover the entire state.

In 1986, he moved to California and became the editor of *Mother Jones*, a liberal political magazine. He was sacked, after just four months, for refusing to print an article that was critical of the Sandinista human rights record in Nicaragua. Moore stated that he would not run the piece because Ronald Reagan "could easily hold it up, saying, 'See, even *Mother Jones* agrees with me'."

Sometimes known as Michael, **Michele Soavi** is an Italian filmmaker. Born in Milan in 1957, he started out acting in films such as *Alien 2* and *City of the Living Dead* before moving to the other side of the camera as assistant director for a Bill Wyman video and on Terry Gilliam's *The Adventures of Baron Munchausen* in 1988.

He left the industry to care for his ill son but returned to work on a feature film, *Catacombs Club*, in 2008.

In his thirtieth year, **Michael Wadleigh** – the American movie director and cinematographer – made a name for himself with the groundbreaking documentary of the infamous 1969 American festival; *Woodstock*.

Released in 1970 and costing $600,000, the finished film is said to have consisted of about 120 miles of footage which was edited down to 184 minutes.

Three of **Michael Winterbottom**'s films, *Welcome to Sarajevo*, *Wonderland* and *24-Hour Party People* – which documents the drug fuelled rise and fall of the influential label Factory Records, and the music scene in Manchester from the late 1970s to the mid-1990s – have been nominated for the Palme d'Or at the Cannes Film Festival. The prolific British filmmaker's first theatrical film, 1995's *Butterfly Kiss*, established his naturalistic style, intense visual sense and compelling use of pop songs to reinforce narrative.

The story of a mentally unbalanced lesbian serial killer and her submissive lover/accomplice falling in love as they slaughter their way across the motorways of northern England managed only a limited release.

His many credits include *Go Now* (1995), *Welcome to Sarajevo* (1997), *Wonderland* (1999) and *Code 46* (2003).

Michael Winner – who once bedded a former *Grange Hill* actress – is now more famous for his insurance advertisements than his film-making.

Born in London into a wealthy family of Jewish expatriates, his Russian father George was a successful property owner while his Polish mother Helen lost an estimated £12 million through compulsive gambling. Born in 1935, Winner compiled 'Michael Winner's Showbiz Gossip' in the *Kensington Post* aged just 14.

In the early 1960s, Winner emerged as a 'hip' film director. His sex comedy *The System* (1964) began a partnership with actor Oliver Reed that would last for six films over a 25-year period. He accepted Charles Bronson's request to film *Death Wish II*, a sequel to the 1974 blockbuster, in 1982. Marlon Brando once said of Winner: "He's the only person I've ever met who talks to me as I wish to be talked to."

Mike Hodges (b. 1932) began his career as a current affairs producer for Granada Television's *World in Action* before moving into feature films.

The screenwriter and film director's credits include *Get Carter* (1971), *Damien: Omen II* (1977 – uncredited), *Flash Gordon* (1980), *Croupier* (1998) and *I'll Sleep When I'm Dead* (2003).

Born in Salford in 1943, **Mike Leigh** is an English film and theatre director, screenwriter, and playwright renowned for his improvised approach to film-making. Leigh begins projects without a script. He sets out a basic premise, and lets the ideas develop through improvisation by the actors, who explore their character.

Most of his films are set amidst the blighted "urban decay of the inner city, or amid the soullessness of suburbia".

His works include *Bleak Moments* (1971), *Abigail's Party* (BBC *Play for Today*, 01/11/1977), *Life Is Sweet* (1990), *Naked* (1993), *All or Nothing* (2002), *Vera Drake* (2004) and *Happy-Go-Lucky* (2008).

Leigh once famously said: "Given the choice of Hollywood or poking steel pins in my eyes, I'd prefer steel pins."

⟫•◦•⟪

MICHAEL JONES IN FOOTBALL

There have been at least three **Michael Joneses** in English professional football.

Mick Jones (born 1945 in Worksop) played 253 minutes for England in three games. The burly forward netted 63 times in 149 appearances for Sheffield United from 1963 to 1967 before winning two league championships with Leeds United.

Mick Jones (b. 1947 in Sunderland) played at centre-back for Derby County – then managed by Brian Clough – Notts County, Peterborough United and Ottawa Tigers in Canada.

Midfielder **Mike Jones** (b. 1987) came through the youth ranks with Tranmere Rovers, spent 13 games on loan at Shrewsbury Town, and as at October 2008 plays for Bury.

WHAT DOES MIKE MEAN, EXACTLY?

(www.urbandictionary.com)

A **Mike** is a person people make fun of you for liking. If
you like a Mike you will get unceremoniously mocked by
your peers. The girls who profess any sort of feelings for a
Mike won't own up for fear of judgement from peers.

This is someone who is easily made fun of by the opposite
sex due to his situation in life; his looks and his lack of luck.

USAGE:
*"I liked Mike until other females found out about it. They warned
me I would be committing 'social suicide' if I were to date a chap as
unattractive and unaccomplished as Mike."*

⟩⟩◆⟨⟨

FOOTBALL CLUB OWNING MICHAELS

Mike Ashley is the billionaire owner of Newcastle United
football club. According to *The Sunday Times* Rich List 2008,
the sports retailer was the 54th richest person in the United
Kingdom sandwiched between Lord and Nat Rothschild,
and Viscount Portman.

Starting with Sport and Ski shops in and around London,
the Buckinghamshire-born entrepreneur gradually
expanded by purchasing Sports World, Lillywhites and
stakes in JJB Sports and JD Sports, to name but a few, as
well as sports brands Donnay, Dunlop Slazenger, Karrimor,
Kangol and Lonsdale.

Previously perceived as somewhat of a recluse, Ashley tried to buy a pint of lager for every Newcastle fan in the away end at Sunderland's Stadium of Light in November 2007 – the stewards stopped him.

Michael Knighton once tried to take over Manchester United for £20 million in 1989. Once monitored by 22 professional clubs, Knighton's early footballing promise was shattered by a career-ending thigh injury while on the ground staff at Coventry City. He gained an FA coaching badge and bought up properties in the Channel Islands before his ambitious plans for the Old Trafford club.

He famously juggled a ball, bedecked in a full home kit, in front of the Stretford End to publicise his intentions. He then tried his luck for a decade at Carlisle United. During this time the Cumbrian club were relegated to the Conference and Knighton claimed to see UFOs.

HOLLYWOOD WALK OF FAME MICHAELS

The Hollywood Walk of Fame is a pavement along Hollywood Boulevard and Vine Street in Hollywood, California.

It features more than 2,000 five-pointed stars featuring the names of not only human celebrities but also fictional characters honoured by the Hollywood Chamber of Commerce for their contributions to the entertainment industry. The first star, awarded on February 9th, 1960, went to Joanne Woodward.

The **Michaels** listed below show the address and type – Motion Pictures (MP); Television (TV); Radio/Recording (Rec) or Live Theatre/Live Performance (LT) – of star received:

Michael Ansara – TV – 6666 Hollywood Boulevard
Michael Bolton – Rec – 7018 Hollywood Boulevard
Michael Collins – TV – Hollywood & Vine
Michael Curtiz – MP – 6640 Hollywood Boulevard
Michael D. Eisner – MP – 6834 Hollywood Boulevard
Michael J. Fox – MP – 7021 Hollywood Boulevard
Mickey Gilley – Rec – 6930 Hollywood Boulevard
Michael Jackson – Radio – 1541 Vine Street
Michael Jackson – Rec – 6927 Hollywood Boulevard
Michael Landon – TV – 1500 N. Vine Street
Al Michaels – TV – 6633 Hollywood Boulevard
Lorne Michaels – TV – 6627 Hollywood Boulevard
Mickey Mouse – MP – 6925 Hollywood Boulevard
Michael O'Shea – TV – 1680 Vine Street
Jan & **Mickey Rooney** – LT – 6801 Hollywood Boulevard
Mickey Rooney – MP – 1718 Vine Street
Mickey Rooney – Radio – 6372 Hollywood Boulevard
Mickey Rooney – TV – 6541 Hollywood Boulevard
Michael York – MP – 6385 Hollywood Boulevard

PLAY-OFF FINAL MICHAELS

The play-offs have been the thrilling climax to the season in the second, third and fourth tiers of professional football in England since the 1986/87 campaign.

Liverpudlian **Mike Newell** scored the only goal in Blackburn Rovers' Division One Play-Off final win over Leicester City at Wembley in May, 1992 to secure their place in the inaugural Premier League.

Former England international **Mike Summerbee**'s son Nicky scored Sunderland's fourth goal, in extra time, in the 1998 Division One Play-Off final against Charlton Athletic. The game finished 4-4 and the Londoners earned promotion with a 7-6 victory on penalties.

Michael Ricketts netted with a minute remaining to earn his Bolton Wanderers side a place in the top flight after a 3-0 win over Lancashire rivals Preston North End at the Millennium Stadium, Cardiff in 2001.

HOWZAT MICHAEL?

Voted at number 32 in the *timesonline* top 50 of Great British losers, **Mike Atherton** (b. 1968, Manchester) was England cricket captain for a record 54 Test matches.

He made his debut against Australia in 1989 and was implicated in a ball-tampering controversy versus South Africa at Lord's in the winter of 1993/94. Plagued by a chronic back condition, Atherton retired after the 2001 Ashes. He played county cricket for Lancashire for 14 years.

Left-handed batsman **Michael Gwyl Bevan** (b. 1970) retired from cricket in January 2007 due to injury. "It got to the stage where injuries and pain were holding back my motivation, and it got to the stage where I was finding it hard to get up for matches and that was probably a pretty clear indication that it was time to move on," said the Australian.

He played 232 One-Day Internationals for his country and was a part of the 1999 and 2003 teams that won the World Cup. Bevan had an exceptional average of over 58.

Born in Lancashire in 1974, former England captain **Michael Vaughan** has represented Yorkshire since 1993. He made his Test debut versus South Africa on 25th November 1999.

As a youngster, Vaughan turned up to watch Yorkshire playing at Sheffield. During the tea break, he was playing on the outfield with his friends when Yorkshire head coach

Doug Padgett spotted him, and approached him about joining the county.

He was born 'over the border' and at the time the county had a strict policy of only picking players that were born in Yorkshire. Years later, when the rule was changed, Padgett sought out the young player and offered him a place at the Yorkshire academy…

Sri Lankan-born **Michael Graydon Vandort** is a left-handed batsman and a right-arm medium-pace bowler and stands at 6ft 5ins. tall.

He scored a century in his country's defeat to England in May 2006 and nearly became the first batsmen since Javed Omar in 2001 to 'carry the bat' – where the opening batsman is 'not out' when the innings is over – through the whole innings.

Mike Gatting (b. 1957) scored 6,504 runs for England and over 50,000 for Middlesex during a career that spanned over 23 years.

He was hit full on the nose by West Indies' Malcolm Marshall during a one-day match in 1984. The fast bowler later found shards of Gatting's nose embedded in the leather. England lost the series 5-0.

His brother Steve enjoyed a long career with Brighton & Hove Albion and played in the 1983 FA Cup Final.

Gatting appeared as himself on *The Archers* on September 9th, 2007 at the centre of a misunderstanding between Sid and Jolene Perks during the Village Cup Final at Lord's.

New Zealander **Michael Shrimpton** played ten Tests for his country from 1963 to 1974 but only took five wickets. He coached the New Zealand women's cricket team to victory in the Women's World Cup in 2000.

With an unorthodox bowling action that generated late in-swing which, in the right conditions, could be unplayable, **Michael Procter**'s powers were noticeably absent from the international cricket scene.

His rise to prominence coincided with South Africa's effective ban from international cricket for two decades from 1971.

He did, however, represent Gloucestershire, as their overseas player, for 13 years, and endeared himself to the home crowd so much they rechristened the side 'Proctershire'.

Michael Holding (b. 1954) is a former West Indian cricketer who was one of the quickest bowlers ever to play Test cricket. Nicknamed 'Whispering Death' by umpires due to his quiet approach to the bowling crease, Holding used skills acquired from running the 400 metres to perfect one of the longest and most rhythmic run-ups in the game.

According to an urban myth – during a Test match against England when Holding was to bowl to Peter Willey – commentator Brian Johnston described the moment thus: "The bowler's Holding, the batsman's Willey."

However, cricket bible *Wisden* states that there is no record of Johnston, or anyone else, actually saying it.

——◆——

MICHAELS BORN IN 1900

Mikhail Fyodorovich Astangov
– Russian actor.
Mikhail Pavlovich Butusov
– Russian football player and coach.
Michael Colbert
– Irish Fianna Fáil politician and farmer.
Monsignor George Michael Crennan AO OBE
– Australian Catholic cleric.
Michael Donnellan
– Irish Clann na Talmhan politician.
Mikhail Efimovich Katukov
– commander of armoured Red Army troops.
Michael Head
– British composer, pianist, organist and singer.
Mikhail Alekseevich Lavrentyev
– Russian mathematician and hydrodynamicist.
Michael Llewelyn Davies
– inspiration for Peter Pan and The Lost Boys.
Count Michael Anthony Maurice de la Bédoyère
– editor, author and journalist.
George Michael O'Neil
– professional baseball player (catcher).

Mikhail Klavdievich Tikhonravov
– Russian pioneer of spacecraft design and rocketry.
Michael Trappes-Lomax
– poet, soldier, historian, and officer of arms.
Mikhail Ivanovich Zharov
– Russian actor.

APRES SKI MICHAEL

The infamous 'curse' of the Kennedy family struck again in 1997 when **Michael LeMoyne** – son of Robert F. Kennedy (assassinated in 1968) and nephew of John F. Kennedy (assassinated in 1963) – died in a skiing accident in Aspen, USA.

One of eleven children, Michael was apparently skiing with several other Kennedy family members when he hit a tree. He was not wearing a helmet, or other safety equipment.

The youngest son of the late Canadian Prime Minister Pierre Trudeau, **Michel Trudeau** (1975-1998) was killed in an avalanche while skiing at British Columbia's Kokanee Glacier Provincial Park. His body was never found.

WHAT A WAY TO GO

Along with his wife Roberta, **Michael Findlay** directed and produced numerous sexploitation films. They are notable for making the infamous *Flesh* trilogy, and *Snuff* (1975).

On May 16th 1977, Findlay – who had ten aliases including Mike and Michael Fenway – was decapitated, although not according to some reports, when the helicopter he was due to board tipped on its side while the rotors were still running.

⇒·◆·⇐

PICKLED MICHAELS

Named in honour of **Mickey Cochrane**, the Hall of Fame catcher from the Philadelphia Athletics, Mickey Mantle (1931-1995) enjoyed an 18-year baseball career with the New York Yankees.

Along with his wife and four sons, Mantle was an alcoholic. He won the World Series seven times.

Michael Elphick died of a heart attack, brought on by years of drinking spirits, in 2002, aged 55.

The popular actor appeared in the classic film *Quadrophenia* and became a household name after appearing in *Boon*. The TV show featured Elphick as Ken, an ex-fireman who was retired from the service after inhaling toxic smoke on a shout, eventually finding work as a courier, minder and private investigator.

MICHAEL

The phrase "he's got the constitution of an ox" could have been inspired by **Mike Malloy**. In 1933, and according to urban legend, he survived numerous murder attempts by a group of men who plotted an elaborate insurance scam.

Money was tight – unemployment stood at 50% – in post-prohibition New York City. Anthony Marino owned a speakeasy in the Bronx and, along with barman Joe Murphy, undertaker Frank Pasqua and friend Dan Kriesberg, devised a plot to take out policies on drunks and then hasten their deaths with alcohol.

Alcoholism had prevented 50-year-old former fireman and engineer Malloy from holding down regular jobs. It was only a matter of time before he drank himself to death, so the men thought. He began to receive free drinks and willingly signed a petition – actually an insurance form – to help 'elect' Marino to local office.

Weeks – and copious free drinks – passed and Malloy seemed fine. The men gave him some "new stuff" which Malloy suggested was "smooth" before crashing to the floor. An hour later he recovered, seemingly oblivious to the anti-freeze! Over the next few days turpentine and even horse liniment laced with rat poison couldn't finish him off.

Even being doused in water and dumped in a snow heap – coatless – in a park in the middle of winter proved fruitless. Next evening he turned up at the bar wearing a new suit procured from the welfare! Exasperated, the gang hired a cab driver to run Malloy down.

For days nothing appeared in the newspapers. It transpired he was recovering in the hospital under a different name, having sustained a fractured skull, concussion and a broken shoulder. He returned to the speakeasy and the men decided to hire a hit man. The fee was too high so they harangued another alcoholic, Joe Murray, got him hideously drunk, placed Malloy's identification in his pocket and ran him over with a taxi.

Murray recovered from his injuries after two months in hospital. The only way to eradicate Malloy, the men concluded, was murder. After drinking whiskey and wood alcohol, a stupendously drunk Malloy's mouth was stuffed with a towel, and a hose connected to a gas jet. It finally worked.

At trial the four murderers either claimed insanity or shifted the blame to each other and died in the electric chair at Sing Sing prison in the summer of 1934.

⇒◆⇐

WHAT DOES MIKE MEAN, EXACTLY?
(www.urbandictionary.com)

It is the art of stubbing out a cigarette just after taking it from another person without having the common decency to ask if they still wish to smoke it.

USAGE:
*"I stopped him just in time… he was about to pull a **Mike** on my last cigarette."*

MORE FOOTBALLERS CALLED MICHAEL

Mike Keeping (1902-1984) played over 200 games at right-back for both Southampton and Fulham before hanging up his boots in 1939. After World War II he managed Spanish giants Real Madrid for a couple of seasons.

Once dubbed the 'The Ryan Giggs of non-league football', **Michael Kightly** (b. 1986) started out as a schoolboy for Tottenham Hotspur and was signed by Wolverhampton Wanderers, from Grays Athletic, in 2006.

Goalkeeper **Mike Kelly** (b. 1942) made 116 appearances in the Football League for Queens Park Rangers and Birmingham City. He was England goalkeeping coach from 1984 to 1990 and worked with the team in two World Cups.

Mike Marsh (b. 1969) made his name at Liverpool in the early 1990s. The midfielder received an insurance pay-out for an injury sustained while playing for Southend United in 1998. As a result he could no longer play league football and spent five years plying his trade outside the top four divisions.

Son of former Manchester City player Alan Oakes, **Michael Oakes** (b. 1973), played 199 times in goal for Wolverhampton Wanderers. He joined Cardiff City in 2007.

Michael James Owen was born on December 14th, 1979 in Chester, Cheshire. The striker has scored over 100 top-flight goals for Liverpool, is one of England's highest ever goalscorers, and scored a hat-trick against Germany on September 1st, 2001.

English-Serbian **Mike Pejic** (b. 1950 in Staffordshire) was a defender with Stoke City, Everton and Aston Villa. He earned eight caps playing for England's under-23s squad and four more with the senior side. He was allegedly dropped by new caretaker England manager Joe Mercer because he "didn't smile enough".

Mike Renshaw (b. 1948 in Manchester) was a left winger. He left Blackpool for Dallas Tornado, of the North American Soccer League, in 1968 after answering a newspaper advertisement looking for young players interested in moving to the US. He played twice for the American national side.

Micky Quinn, (b. 1962) was a prolific striker who scored over 200 league goals for Wigan Athletic, Stockport County, Oldham Athletic, Portsmouth, Newcastle United and Coventry City. While at Portsmouth the fans' chant for him was: "He's fat, he's round, he's worth a million pound, Micky Quinn, Micky Quinn!"

EYES IN THE BACK OF YOUR HEAD, MICHAEL

Sir Michael Francis O'Dwyer was the sixth of 14 children and was the Lieutenant Governor of the Punjab, India from 1912 until 1919.

On April 13th 1919, thousands of Sikhs had gathered in Amritsar for Baisakhi, an annual religious festival. Under the command of Brigadier General Reginald Dyer, ninety Gurkha soldiers opened fire on the unarmed crowd.

Three days earlier riots had broken out following O'Dwyer's expulsion of two Indian nationalists. Five Englishmen had been murdered and an Englishwoman left for dead, and banks and public buildings had been looted and burnt.

The Jallianwala Bagh Massacre, according to official figures, claimed 379 unarmed civilians, including a six-week old baby. Just over twenty years later, at a meeting of the Royal Central Asian Society in Caxton Hall, London on March 13th 1940, O'Dwyer was shot dead by Punjabi revolutionary, Udham Singh, in retaliation for the massacre. His killer was hanged... with a smile from ear to ear.

Count **Mikhail Andreyevich Miloradovich** (1771-1825) was a prominent Russian general during the Napoleonic wars.

He was military governor of Saint Petersburg from 1818 onwards and on December 26th, 1825 he went to pacify the Decembrist officers – the Decembrist revolt took place as Russian army officers led about 3,000 soldiers in a protest against Nicholas I's assumption of the throne after his elder brother Constantine removed himself from the line of succession – at the Senate Square. Miloradovich almost succeeded when one of the more radical rebels, Pyotr Kakhovsky, shot him dead.

TITANIC MICHAELS

On the night of April 14th 1912, during her maiden voyage, *Titanic* – built at the Harland and Wolff shipyard in Belfast – hit an iceberg, and sank two hours and forty minutes later, early on April 15th 1912.

The disaster claimed 1,500 lives. The ship did not carry enough lifeboats for everyone aboard and had a total lifeboat capacity of 1,178, even though her maximum capacity was 3,547 people. A women-and-children-first protocol was followed.

Here are the lost Michaels on board that fateful evening…

Slovakian tailor **Michel Navratil** married Marcelle Caretto in 1907. They had two sons, Master Michel M. and Edmond Roger. By 1912 the business was in trouble and Michel claimed that his wife Marcelle had been having an affair.

After the couple separated, the boys went to stay with their father over the Easter weekend but when Marcelle came to collect them, they had disappeared.

The 32-year-old decided to take the boys to America and purchased second class tickets (ticket No.230080, £26) for the *Titanic* at Southampton. His children were booked in as Loto and Louis and he used the name 'Louis M. Hoffman'.

On the night of the sinking Second Officer Charles Lightoller ordered a locked-arms circle of crew members around Collapsible D (lifeboat) so that only women and children could get through. Michel handed the boys through the ring of men and fellow passenger Margaret Hays took care of them.

Michel Jr. recalled that just before placing him in the boat, his father gave a final message: "My child, when your mother comes for you, as she surely will, tell her that I loved her dearly and still do. Tell her I expected her to follow us, so that we might all live happily together in the peace and freedom of the New World."

His body was recovered (#15) with a revolver in the pocket.

Michael Connaghton, 31, was visiting relatives in Ballymahon, Ireland and was returning to his home in Brooklyn, New York after boarding at Queenstown.

Michael Linehan, 21, of Boherboy, Ireland boarded the *Titanic* at Queenstown as a third class passenger (ticket number 330971, £7 17s 7d) with Daniel Buckley, Hannah Riordan, Bridget Bradley, Patrick Denis O'Connell, Patrick O'Connor and Nora O'Leary.

His body, if recovered, was never identified.

Farm labourer **Michael McEvoy** (McElroy), aged 19, of Dublin, Ireland boarded the *Titanic* at Queenstown as a third class passenger (ticket number 36568, £7 10s) and died in the disaster.

Michael Kieran, 31, was born in Lancaster and, as a storekeeper on the ship, he received monthly wages of £3 15s. According to Frank Prentice, he, Kieran and fellow assistant storekeeper Cyril Ricks jumped from the stern in the final moments of the sinking.

Michael Croughane, 42, was part of the *Titanic* Engineering Crew as a Engine Stoker and boarded at Belfast. **Michael Rogers**, 27, of the *Titanic* Victualling Crew was employed as a Saloon Steward and boarded the doomed the ship at Southampton. Both perished.

Rescuers

The *Carpathia* was sailing from New York City to Rijeka, Croatia on the night of Sunday, 14 April 1912. On receiving a distress signal from the *Titanic*, Captain Arthur Henry Rostron immediately set a course at maximum speed to the stricken ship's last known position, approximately 58 miles away. He ordered the ship's heating and hot water to be cut off so the engines could feed on every ounce of steam.

At 4am *Carpathia* arrived at the scene after working her way through dangerous ice fields and saved 705 people.

"There are all kinds of ways to get dead in a shipwreck."
Michael H. Standart

There was some good news...

Michael J. Joseph was born in Detroit, Michigan on May 11th 1907, the son of Lebanese immigrants. Along with his mother and sister the youngster boarded the *Titanic* at Cherbourg as a third class passenger.

After the sinking Michael saw a great number of icebergs in the water, a scene that haunted him for the rest of his life. He was reunited with his mother on the *Carpathia*.

Michael worked as a delivery boy for a soft drinks company for many years, married and raised a family in his hometown. He was not keen to discuss the disaster, but would do so occasionally with his grandson Brian.

He died on 18 May 1991. On his gravestone is a small painting of the *Titanic*.

What does Mike mean, exactly?

(www.urbandictionary.com)

Slang from the American prohibition era, used as a casual address.

It is similar to London's 'mate', or Newcastle's 'man', and much like New York's modern-day 'dude'.

USAGE:
"Say there, can you answer me another question, ***Mike****?"*
"I can't, and my name ain't Mike."

Curling Michaels

Michael and Mikes have featured regularly in the medal tables at the World Curling Championships but only one has picked up a gold.

The most decorated man in world curling is **Mike Hay** with five medals to his name, including gold in 1991, in his Scottish homeland.

Mike Slyziuk (USA) – 1963 (B)
Mike O'Leary (USA) – 1966 (B)

Mike Chernoff (Canada) – 1978 (B)
Michael Sindt (Denmark) – 1985 (B)
Mikael Hasselborg (Sweden) – 1985 (S)
Mike Hay (Scotland) – 1986 (S), 1988 (B), 1990 (S), 1991 (G), 1997 (B)
Mikael Ljungberg (Sweden) – 1989 (B), 1994 (S)
Mike Fraboni (USA) – 1991 (B)
Michael Schäffer (Germany) – 1994 (B); 1997 (S)
Jean-Michel Ménard (Canada) – 2006 (S)

(B) = Bronze; (S) = Silver; (G) = Gold

———◆———

WHAT DOES MICHAEL MEAN, EXACTLY?

(www.urbandictionary.com)

A large bowling ball-shaped boy, with a hair colour that makes one think he has a turd on his head.

USAGE:
*"Hey, there goes **Michael**, he looks like he has a turd on his head. Yeah, like a bowling ball that rolled through pooh."*

GONE TOO EARLY

Michael Lee Alfonso (1965-2007), better known
by his ring name Mike Awesome, was an American
professional wrestler. Standing at 6ft 7ins. he was Extreme
Championship Wrestling World Heavyweight Champion
twice in 1999 and announced his retirement from wrestling
seven years later saying he wanted to spend more time with
his family. He stated that he would only return to the ring
"if the money was right".

Awesome was found hanged in his Tampa home on
February 17th 2007.

Father of six **Micke Dubois** was a Swedish actor and
comedian who began his career as an air-guitarist. In 1988
the portly funnyman launched the character of Svullo – a
taunt name for obese people in his home country – and
formed a duo with Hans Crispin; Angne & Svullo.

Dubois committed suicide by hanging, aged 46, in
November 2005.

His mother survived Auschwitz and his father was a survivor
from the Russian front. **Mike Brant** (born Moshe Brand,
1947) had an inauspicious start himself, coming into the world
at midnight in an Israelite refugee camp in Famagusta, Cyprus.

He remained mute until the age of five when his first word
was "kerach", ice in Hebrew. By the time he was 11, Brant

was the only boy in his school choir. With four friends, he formed a band, The Chocolates, and sang at parties and clubs around Tel Aviv and Haifa. They were signed in 1968 and toured the USA for a year before a chance meeting with Sylvie Vartan, who invited him to Paris. He soon had a hit with Let Me Love You.

By 1973, he was performing 250 concerts a year. This went on for two years and he suffered depression and loneliness. On November 22nd 1974 he jumped out the window of his manager's fifth floor hotel room in Geneva, only to land on a balcony two levels down. He broke bones but survived.

On April 25th 1975, the day his new album was released, Brant eventually succeeded in killing himself by leaping to his death from an apartment in Paris. He was 28.

French psychologist and statistician **Michel Gauquelin** conducted statistical research on astrology and concentrated on affirming the existence of a correlation between:

- the positions of the planets
- the day of an individual's birth
- the psychological character and the effect of this character upon their destiny

"On the whole, it emerged that there was an increasingly solid statistical link between the time of birth of great men and their occupational success… Having collected over 20,000 dates of birth of professional celebrities from various European countries and from the United States, I had to draw the unavoidable conclusion that the position of the planets at birth is linked to one's destiny. What a challenge to the rational mind!" (*Neo-Astrology*, 1991)

He took his own life, aged 62, in 1991.

Michael Gilden played an Ewok in *Star Wars Episode VI: Return of the Jedi* and also performed in other productions including; *Charmed*, *CSI: Crime Scene Investigation*, *Cybill* and *Pulp Fiction*.

Gilden stood at 4ft 6ins. and also worked as a financial advisor. In 2006, aged just 44, the American actor committed suicide.

On November 22nd 2008, the remaining members of INXS paid tribute to former lead singer **Michael Hutchence**, on the tenth anniversary of his death. The 37-year-old Australian was found hanged in a Sydney hotel room.

The one-time partner of Bob Geldof's ex-wife Paula Yates and famous for hits which included Need You Tonight and Mystify, the vocalist's untimely passing prompted his friend, Duran Duran's Simon Le Bon, to pen these lyrics:

"Trust you to get caught up in somebody's war; you'll come out of it all intact, I'm sure. Just remember what friends were put here for; ***Michael****, you've got a lot to answer for, and I know that you're gonna call... if you need me."*

American drummer **Michael Clarke** was in The Byrds from 1964 to 1968. He ran away from home when he was 17 years old and hitchhiked to California to become a musician.

Clarke was reportedly hired more for his resemblance to Rolling Stones guitarist Brian Jones than his musical skills. After years of bitter wrangling over the use of the band's name, Clarke died of liver failure, aged 47, in 1994 after three decades of alcohol abuse.

Australian poet **Michael Dransfield** (b. 1948) was active in the 1960s and early 1970s.

He wrote his first poem at the age of eight and his work began to focus more and more on drug experiences as he got older.

An active protester against the Vietnam War, he was conscripted but excused for health reasons.

His poems were published in *Meanjin* (pronounced *Mee-AN-jin* – derived from an Aboriginal word for the land where the city of Brisbane is located), *Poetry Australia* and *Poetry* magazine (a 30,000 subscriber publication that has been funded by a $200m donation from American philanthropist Ruth Lilly since 2003).

Dransfield exchanged poems with Peter Kocan – who had been imprisoned for attempting to assassinate federal opposition leader Arthur Calwell, who was then a mental patient – and regularly explored issues related to the fragility of human relationships and drug use.

He died, aged 24, in 1973. The coroner's report suggested the cause of death was "acute broncho-pneumonia and brain damage" whereas some sources claim a heroin overdose.

Dransfield left a thousand poems.

ON THIS DAY MICHAELS

<u>Christmas Day</u>

1261 – **Michael VIII Palaeologus**
deposed and blinded his co-ruler, John IV Lascaris of the
restored Eastern Roman Empire, on his 11th birthday

1991 – **Mikhail Gorbachev**
resigned as president of the Soviet Union (the union itself is
dissolved the next day)

Michaels born:

1907 – Mike Mazurki, Ukrainian-born actor (d. 1990)
1945 – Mike Pringle, Scottish politician
1959 – Michael P. Anderson, astronaut (d. 2003)

<u>New Year's Day</u>

Michaels born:

1960 – Michael Seibert, American ice dancer
1968 – Miki Higashino, Japanese composer
1984 – Michael Witt, Australian rugby league footballer

Michaels died:

1862 – Mikhail Ostrogradsky, Russian physicist (b. 1801)
1919 – Mikhail Drozdovsky, Russian general (b. 1881)
1956 – Mike Mitchell, American basketball player

Valentine's Day – February 14th

Michaels born:

1934 – Michel Corboz, Swiss conductor
1942 – Michael Bloomberg, Mayor of New York City
1962 – Michael Higgs, English actor
1986 – Michael Ammermüller, German racing driver

Michaels died:

1995 – Michael V. Gazzo, American actor (b. 1923)

Mountaineering Michaels

Mount Everest is the highest mountain on planet Earth with its summit 8,848 metres (29,029 ft) above sea level. Many climbers have attempted, and failed, to conquer the impressive peak.

The following climbers perished on the slopes of the great mountain:

1975 – Mick Burke
1996 – Mike Rheinberger
1999 – Mike Matthews
2005 – Mike O'Brien

"Calm down dear, it's only a commercial".
Michael Winner's *quote on a British TV advert*

———❦———

BIT TOO FAST MICHAEL!

Rally driver **Michael Park** died – aged 39 in 2005 – as a result of injuries sustained when his vehicle left the road and struck a tree during the final leg of Wales Rally Great Britain.

'Beef' enjoyed success in Estonia after teaming up with Markko Märtin. A statue in his honour was unveiled in the capital, Tallinn, in 2006.

Italian racing driver **Michele Alboreto** is famous for finishing runner up to Alain Prost in the 1985 Formula One World Championship. His career in motorsport began in 1976, racing a car he and his friends had built in the Formula Monza series. In 2001, aged 44, he was killed testing an Audi at the Lausitzring in Germany.

Mike Burgmann (1947-1986) died when he lost control of his race car while travelling at 268 km/h. He was driving over the second hump on Conrod Straight before he collided with a tyre barrier at the base of the Bridgestone Bridge during the Bathurst 100 at the Mount Panorama Circuit in New South Wales.

Mike Spence began his motor sport career through involvement with his family's garage business in Maidenhead, Berkshire in 1958. Within five years he was called up to the Lotus Formula One team.

From the 1964 British Grand Prix onwards Spence moved up to partner Scot Jim Clark – who won 25 out of 73 races – in the Formula One team.

After Clark's death in early 1968, Spence was invited to take part in the Indianapolis 500. During practice at the Indianapolis Motor Speedway, three weeks before his first race, the Croydon-born driver misjudged a turn and collided heavily with the concrete wall.

The right front wheel of the vehicle entered the cockpit and struck Spence on the helmet.

He died in the hospital, from massive head injuries, a few hours after the accident.

WHAT DOES MICK MEAN, EXACTLY?
(www.urbandictionary.com)

Noun: an action done with complete thoughtlessness.
Verb: to commit a **Mick**.

Origin: "Mick", truncation of "Mickey".

USAGE:
1. *"Did that fat bastard scoff another cake?"*
"Yeah, she's prone to Micks."
2. *"Ah, Elaine Micked again! She left the back door open in the rain!"*

━━━◆━━━

LOVE MICHAEL

Michael Stich won the Wimbledon Men's Singles title in
1991 beating fellow countryman Boris Becker 6-4, 7-6, 6-4.
The German, born in 1968, enjoyed 18 career title wins,
and finished runner-up on 13 occasions.

At the age of 17 years and 3 months, Chinese American
Michael Chang won the French Open title in 1989. He
beat Swede Stefan Edberg in a five-set final, winning 6-1,
3-6, 4-6, 6-4, 6-2. He was victorious in 34 tournaments and
was a beaten finalist 24 times.

He now coaches his wife, **Amber Christine Liu** (b. 1984),
who was ranked 241 in the world as at March 2009.

Left-handed Frenchman **Michaël Llodra** – whose father Michel played football for Paris Saint-Germain – won the Wimbledon Men's Doubles title, with partner Arnaud Clément, in 2007.

Mike Belkin (b. 1945) was Canada's top-ranked player five times between 1966 and 1972.

Mike Bryan (b. 1978), along with twin brother Bob, is an American professional tennis player. The pair have won the following Grand Slam tournaments; Australian Open – 2006, 2007, 2009; French Open – 2003; Wimbledon – 2006; US Open – 2005, 2008.

Australian Rules Michael

Michael Braun (b. 1978) – West Coast Eagles.

Michael Brennan (b. 1965) – West Coast Eagles. Won Premierships in 1992 and 1994 – was named in their Team of the Decade

Michael Bowden (b. 1947) – Richmond Football Club. Has three sons who have also represented the Tigers

Michael Byrne (b. 1958) – Melbourne, Hawthorn and Sydney.

Michael Mansfield (b. 1971) – Geelong.
Twice named an All Australian – an all-star team selected
by a panel at the end of each season – in 1994 and 1995

Michael Green (b. 1948) – Richmond.
Now runs Greens List, one of Victoria's largest barristers'
clerk services

Michael Hurley (b. 1990) – Essendon.

Michael Warren (b. 1982) – Claremont and Fremantle.

Michael 'Kingo' Taylor (b. 1953) – Collingwood and
Norwood. Inducted, in 2002, into the South Australian
Football Hall of Fame

<hr>

WHAT DOES MIKE MEAN, EXACTLY?
(www.urbandictionary.com)

A **Mike** is a unit of measure, approximately equal to six
feet.

It can only be used to measure the distance travelled from
the point you locked the door, to the point you turned
around to go back into the house, to retrieve what was
forgotten.

USAGE:
Person one: "Back so soon?"
Person two: "Yeah, I went four Mikes and remembered my wallet."

There is every chance we have missed a Michael, or two.

Let us know at **www.stripepublishing.co.uk**

ACKNOWLEDGEMENTS

Firstly, sincere thanks must go to Dave Blake for planting the seed of an idea in a Brighton café back in January 2008.

Chris and Paul deserve a huge amount of credit for believing in me, and the idea, and using their knowledge and expertise to help get the project off the ground.

I must also thank the other authors in the series, in no particular order – Richard Shananan, Paul Reaney, James Whittington, Dave Blake, Stewart Cruttenden, Max Leonard, Jason Dickinson, Paul Geraghty and Andrew Robinson – for their excellent work.

Thanks to Andy Searle, for the great typesetting job, to Jonathan Pugh for his excellent illustrations, and to Dean Rockett for his diligent proofing.

Also, a big "cheers" to Andy Heath for his patience and skill; listen out for Zarbo – great music.

And finally, a massive shout out to Benski, Le Dude, Benz and Rob for being the best office mates anyone could wish for.

BIBLIOGRAPHY

The Book Of Lasts – Cassell Illustrated, Octopus Publishing Group Ltd. (2005)

The Encyclopaedia Britannica – http://www.britannica.com

Top Ten Of Everything 2008, Russell Ash – Octopus Publishing Group Ltd. (2007)

Potty, Fartwell and Knob, Russell Ash – Headline Publishing (2007)

The Heiltsuks: Dialogues of Culture and History on the Northwest Coast, Michael E. Harkin – Lincoln: University of Nebraska Press (1997)

Encyclopedia Titanica – Michael Kieran (2009)

RECOMMENDED WEBSITES

www.grangehillfans.co.uk
www.barrytrotter.com
www.answers.com
www.screenonline.org.uk
www.wikipedia.org
www.forbes.com
www.money.cnn.com
www.crimelibrary.com
www.leunig.com.au
www.chessworld.net
www.nba.com/playerfile
www.pgatour.com.au
www.europeantour.com
www.thepeerage.com
www.embracingthechild.org
www.dhm.de
www.corrie.net
www.scottishfa.co.uk
www.thefa.com
www.urbandictionary.com
www.phrases.org.uk
www.artnet.com
www.rectoversion.com
www.eecs.tufts.edu
www.miguelconde.info
www.bretmichaels.com
www.nytimes.com
www.rigb.org/heritage
www.iomguide.com
www.cbsnews.com

www.michaelendres.com
www.business.timesonline.co.uk
www.thebiographychannel.co.uk
www.news.bbc.co.uk
www.darwinawards.com
www.englandstats.com
www.mikebrant.co.il
www.encyclopedia-titanica.org